CW00616094

WHERE THE WORLD MEETS TO PRAY

Susan Hibbins
UK Editor

INTERDENOMINATIONAL
INTERNATIONAL
INTERRACIAL

36 LANGUAGES
Multiple formats are available in some languages

The Bible Reading Fellowship
15 The Chambers, Vineyard
Abingdon OX14 3FE
brf.org.uk

The Bible Reading Fellowship (BRF) is a Registered Charity (233280)

ISBN 978 0 85746 916 8
All rights reserved

Originally published in the USA by The Upper Room® **upperroom.org**
US edition © 2020 The Upper Room, Nashville, TN (USA). All rights reserved.
This edition © The Bible Reading Fellowship 2020
Cover image © Thinkstock

Acknowledgements

Scripture quotations marked with the following abbreviations are taken from the
version shown. Where no acronym is given, the quotation is taken from the same
version as the headline reference.

NRSV: The New Revised Standard Version of the Bible, Anglicised Edition, copyright
© 1989, 1995 by the Division of Christian Education of the National Council of the
Churches of Christ in the USA. Used by permission. All rights reserved.

NIV: The Holy Bible, New International Version (Anglicised edition) copyright © 1979,
1984, 2011 by Biblica. Used by permission of Hodder & Stoughton Publishers, an
Hachette UK company. All rights reserved. 'NIV' is a registered trademark of Biblica.
UK trademark number 1448790.

CEB: copyright © 2011 by Common English Bible.

KJV: the Authorised Version of the Bible (The King James Bible), the rights in which are
vested in the Crown, are reproduced by permission of the Crown's Patentee, Cambridge
University Press.

A catalogue record for this book is available from the British Library

Printed by Gutenberg Press, Tarxien, Malta

How to use *The Upper Room*

The Upper Room is ideal in helping us spend a quiet time with God each day. Each daily entry is based on a passage of scripture, and is followed by a meditation and prayer. Each person who contributes a meditation to the magazine seeks to relate their experience of God in a way that will help those who use *The Upper Room* every day.

Here are some guidelines to help you make best use of *The Upper Room*:

1 Read the passage of scripture. It is a good idea to read it more than once, in order to have a fuller understanding of what it is about and what you can learn from it.
2 Read the meditation. How does it relate to your own experience? Can you identify with what the writer has outlined from their own experience or understanding?
3 Pray the written prayer. Think about how you can use it to relate to people you know, or situations that need your prayers today.
4 Think about the contributor who has written the meditation. Some users of the *The Upper Room* include this person in their prayers for the day.
5 Meditate on the 'Thought for the day' and the 'Prayer focus', perhaps using them again as the focus for prayer or direction for action.

Why is it important to have a daily quiet time? Many people will agree that it is the best way of keeping in touch every day with the God who sustains us, and who sends us out to do his will and show his love to the people we encounter each day. Meeting with God in this way reassures us of his presence with us, helps us to discern his will for us and makes us part of his worldwide family of Christian people through our prayers.

I hope that you will be encouraged as you use the magazine regularly as part of your daily devotions, and that God will richly bless you as you read his word and seek to learn more about him.

Susan Hibbins
UK Editor

BRF needs you!

If you're one of our thousands of regular *Upper Room* readers you will know all about the rich rewards of regular Bible reading and the value of daily notes to encourage and inspire you. *Upper Room* readers share those blessings with Christians across the world. In the words of UK Editor Susan Hibbins, they know that 'every day, in each part of the day, someone, somewhere is reading the same meditation'.

If you enjoy reading *The Upper Room* and love the feeling of being part of a worldwide family, would you be willing to help spread the word about this popular resource? Could you, for example, start an *Upper Room* reading group to introduce your friends or colleagues to the notes, not to take the place of private prayer and reflection but to share insights and grow together.

It doesn't need to be complicated or nerve-wracking: every reflection in *The Upper Room* ends with a question or thought to ponder. And because these reflections are rooted in the personal experience of Christians from every corner of the world, to read and discuss them with others will help to deepen knowledge, strengthen friendships and forge worldwide bonds of faith and fellowship.

We can supply further information if you need it and would love to hear about it if you do start an *Upper Room* reading group.

For more information:

- Email **enquiries@brf.org.uk**
- Telephone BRF on **+44 (0)1865 319700** Mon–Fri 9.15–17.30
- Write to us at BRF, 15 The Chambers, Vineyard, Abingdon OX14 3FE.

What's the difference?

As you therefore have received Christ Jesus the Lord, continue to live your lives in him, rooted and built up in him… abounding in thanksgiving.
Colossians 2:6–7 (NRSV)

When I was young, I overheard my parents telling other parents that my sister and I were good at choosing friends. They meant that we surrounded ourselves with people who cared about us, supported us and generally made good decisions. Looking back, I am grateful for the friends and community I had as a young person. Those people shaped my worldview, supported me in my journey of faith and helped me become the person I am today. Who we spend time with matters.

A relationship with God through Jesus Christ is much the same. When we take time to pray, read scripture, reflect on our faith and listen for God's leading, our lives are shaped in unique and meaningful ways. In this issue, many writers share stories about the ways that faith in Christ and a dedication to spiritual practices have affected their lives. Some describe shifts in attitude and relationships because of their connection to God. Others describe a new-found sense of peace and awareness of God's presence when they slow down and invest time in practising their faith.

As you read this issue, I invite you to consider what difference a relationship with God makes in your daily life. I hope that you will find new ways to practise and invest in your faith over the coming months.

Lindsay L. Gray
Editorial Director, The Upper Room

Gifts to the international editions of *The Upper Room* help the world meet to pray. **upperroom.org/gift**

Hong Kong
The Methodist Church, Hong Kong, is promoting *The Upper Room* among secondary schools by distributing copies to librarians to share with students.

Japan
The Japanese edition of *The Upper Room* celebrated 70 years of publishing in 2019! They are expanding their readership through promotions and advertisements via SMS text messaging.

Korea
The Korea Christian Leader's Mission, a publisher of *The Upper Room* in Korea, welcomed a new chairman and editor last year.

Editions of *The Upper Room* daily devotional guide are printed in:
- **Hong Kong** (Chinese, Chinese/English)
- **Japan** (Japanese, English)
- **Korea** (Korean, Korean/English and Korean/English/Japanese)

The Editor writes...

It is with some sadness that I write this editorial, since it is my last as UK editor of *The Upper Room* UK edition.

It is now almost 20 years since I first became the editor, and what a privilege it has been to share in the work of The Upper Room, based in Tennessee, and with The Bible Reading Fellowship in the UK. I have so appreciated reading the uplifting stories of faith in the meditations which make up this unique devotional magazine. *The Upper Room* truly represents many individuals who form a worldwide family of faith, people who want to share with others what God is doing in their lives.

In addition, many of the letters and comments I have received over the years say how much a particular meditation has helped them or someone they know; how it spoke to their situation, or trouble, or bereavement, at exactly the right moment. The power of scripture speaks through the meditations, and the words on the page have an authority that is more than just the writer's own. I know that the Holy Spirit will direct the scripture message of each day exactly to where it is needed most.

I believe too that the Holy Spirit can use us and our lives to take the message of scripture out into the world. We only have to be willing, and we will find opportunities to pass on what we have learned, whether at work, in our leisure time or at church. The world has never needed the gospel message as urgently as it does now, and God is relying on us to be his eyes, hands and feet.

As I move into a new chapter of life, I would like to thank you all for the companionship and friendship I have received from you on the way – and may God bless us all with his continuing grace.

Susan Hibbins
UK Editor

The Bible readings are selected with great care, and we urge you to include the suggested reading in your devotional time.

Strength in weakness

Read 2 Corinthians 12:1–10

[The Lord] said to me, 'My grace is sufficient for you, for my power is made perfect in weakness.'
2 Corinthians 12:9 (NIV)

As a nurse in a busy surgical-oncology unit, I was feeling depleted. Slumped into a pew in the quiet hospital chapel, I gazed mindlessly at a group of candles in the corner. One flickered weakly. 'How will I get through this shift, Lord? I feel like that candle – about to burn out.' The verse quoted above flashed through my mind, bringing comfort. Our weakness elicits God's compassion – not his judgement.

Reaching into my pocket for a pen to scribble down my thoughts, I pulled out a latex glove. How useless it seemed! Then, lifting my right hand, I studied its strong tendons and slipped it into the blue glove. The lifeless material was now filled with form and strength. As I opened and closed my gloved fist, God reminded me that I can do all things through Christ who strengthens me (see Philippians 4:13). I left the chapel reassured that God's strength and power within me – not my weakness – would prevail.

God does not ask us to be strong on our own. He asks us to pray and believe that his power is with us. We can trust God to fill us and to equip us for any task the day brings.

Prayer: *Thank you, Lord, for the presence of your Spirit and your power within us this day. Amen*

Thought for the day: When I am weak, I can find strength in God's power.

Dee Aspin (California, US)

Loving one another

Read Luke 6:27–36
'This is my commandment, that you love one another as I have loved you.'
John 15:12 (NRSV)

When I was eleven years old, a new family joined our church. Alex, the 13-year-old boy in this family, was a bit wild, and I mostly avoided him because I thought he was loud and immature. After a few months, my mum told me she had invited Alex and his mum to our house for the afternoon. I was not thrilled by this arrangement, but my mum said it would be a good thing to do for this new family, especially as Alex didn't have many friends. The day came, and Alex and I had fun. From then on I spent a lot of time with him, and to this day he remains one of my closest friends.

God calls us to love all people. I believe he sets up situations like this more frequently than we realise. Now when I find myself not wanting to spend time with someone who is different from me, I think back to when I met Alex and reflect on the blessing that our friendship has been. I remember that God loves me unconditionally. So what excuse do I have not to love those different from me?

Prayer: *Dear God, help us to be open to new friendships and to love others as you love us. Amen*

Thought for the day: God can bless me through unlikely friendships.

Gabe Herman (South Dakota, US)

Searching for peace

Read Psalm 91:1–13

[The Lord] will command his angels concerning you to guard you in all your ways.
Psalm 91:11 (NIV)

Recently, I was going through a difficult time. I went into the church to pray and try to find peace. From the church I admired the birds perched on the leafy trees, and I noticed three large, green lizards there too. The lizards were eating the abundant leaves. Then I remembered that those particular trees have thorns. 'How curious,' I thought. 'The lizards seem fine. How can they manoeuvre around the trees without harming themselves on the thorns?' As I thought more about this, I realised that God had equipped these creatures with a scaly, dry outer layer that protects them.

Then my thoughts turned to today's quoted Bible verse – how reassuring to know that God's angels protect us. God also provides us with prayer and scripture as tools to help us find peace. We can trust that God will protect us and free us from anxiety.

Prayer: *Creator God, sweep away all anxiety and make us new again. Grant us peace in mind, body, soul and spirit. We pray as Jesus taught us, 'Our Father which art in heaven, Hallowed be thy name. Thy kingdom come. Thy will be done, as in heaven, so in earth. Give us day by day our daily bread. And forgive us our sins; for we also forgive every one that is indebted to us. And lead us not into temptation; but deliver us from evil.'* Amen*

Thought for the day: Don't be anxious; present your requests to God (see Philippians 4:6).

Evelyn Jiménez Vélez (Puerto Rico)

PRAYER FOCUS: THOSE I KNOW WHO NEED GOD'S PEACE TODAY
*Luke 11:2–4 (KJV)

In small ways

Read Matthew 25:31–40

'Whatever you did for one of the least of these brothers and sisters of mine, you did for me.'
Matthew 25:40 (NIV)

When I was younger I looked forward to retirement as a time when I would do something great for God. I imagined a missionary journey where I would bring hope to all I would meet. Or I would finally write an important treatise that would capture everyone's heart and save the world.

When I retired two years after cancer treatment, I did not have the energy for either of those dreams. Instead I worked one morning a week serving in my church's food bank, another visiting my mother in the nursing home where she lived and other days volunteering at a local school. But I was disappointed. It didn't seem enough.

Then I remembered the common phrase, 'Bloom where you are planted.' I looked for little ways to share great love. Now I make cards of encouragement for the people who receive food from our food bank. I put together thank-you gifts for the staff at my mother's home. I post a daily prayer online based on my Bible reading.

It is not the size or grandeur of our mission that counts. We can all do something to bring God's grace to the world around us.

Prayer: *Lord of all, lead us to ways to share your love with those around us. Amen*

Thought for the day: I can share God's great love in small ways.

Kim Whitlock Sisk (Oklahoma, US)

God is everywhere

Read Genesis 39:20–23

If I ascend up into heaven, thou art there: if I make my bed in hell, behold, thou art there.
Psalm 139:8 (KJV)

As I grew up, I heard my parents say that God is everywhere. I used to wonder, 'How can God be everywhere when I cannot see him?' But when I started going to church, I began to experience God's presence in every situation.

When I lost my job, I felt God's presence. At times I felt like giving up, but a voice within me kept reminding me that God is faithful. During those trying moments, Joseph's story became real for me. Joseph went through a lot, but God was with him. When he was thrown into a pit (see Genesis 37:24), put in prison (see Genesis 39:20) and finally made a ruler in Egypt (see Genesis 41:40-43), God's presence stayed with him.

In my struggles, I formed the habit of rising early to praise, worship and spend time with God. During those dark moments, his presence and grace were my greatest hope and refuge. I knew that he understood my situation. My family saw the hope I found in God's presence, and they joined me in worship.

A year later, I continued to experience God's presence when I found another job that was better than the one I'd lost. No matter what our situation is, God will not fail us.

Prayer: *Ever-present God, surround us with your presence in every situation. Amen*

Thought for the day: If I look, I can find signs of God's presence all around me.

Benedict Mutweko Musee (Kajiado County, Kenya)

Peace in our hearts

Read Joshua 1:1–9

Who shall separate us from the love of Christ?
hardship or persecution or famine or nakedne
Romans 8:35 (NIV)

I had just returned from the market one morning when I was shocked by a message from my friends. They told me that three churches in our city had been bombed. All the churches in the city had to cancel their services that day, so some of my friends and I agreed to hold our own service at my friend's house. Even in the midst of the chaotic situation, we could praise and worship God, pray and share a sermon. The situation in our city could not prevent us from continuing to praise and worship God.

Through that experience I realised that many things – big and small – can scare us. But even amid fear, we can continue to believe that God is with us no matter what happens. When we pray and put our trust in God, he will give us peace in our hearts. We do not have to fear because when we are with God, we are more than conquerors (see Romans 8:37).

Prayer: *Dear God, we believe that whatever happens, you are still with us. Help us to look beyond our fear and to accept the peace that you offer us. Amen*

Thought for the day: Amid chaos, I can find peace through worshipping God.

Meliana Santoso (East Java, Indonesia)

adfast example

John 13:12–17

have set you an example that you should do as I have done for you.'
John 13:15 (NIV)

As I took out the rubbish one afternoon, I saw a car approaching. The driver rolled down the window and said, 'Hi.' I recognised her as one of my neighbours. She went on to say that she had been diagnosed with cancer, and the doctors were performing tests to see if it had gone to her spine. When I told her I was sorry to hear this news, I tentatively added that I would pray for her. I had never brought up my faith with her, but I felt led to share. She responded, 'I knew you would pray for me. Thank you.' As she went on her way, I praised God. I realised that I had quietly set an example as a Christian to my neighbours – and in doing so had given a word of hope.

Though we may be timid in sharing our faith, we can set an example of what it means to be a Christian. As we set an example through our daily living, God will bring opportunities to share our faith with others. Our opportunities may be a commitment to pray or an invitation to share the gospel. God will direct our paths and the words we speak. Jesus set an example for us through his actions, and we can offer Christian love to others through our actions and words.

Prayer: *Dear heavenly Father, help me to be an example of Christ in my actions and words. In Jesus' name. Amen*

Thought for the day: How will my actions demonstrate my faith today?

Jodi Wheeler (Arizona, US)

The well-marked path

Read Proverbs 4:10–18
This is God, our God forever and ever. He will be our guide forever.
Psalm 48:14 (NRSV)

Hiking in the forests of the Pacific Northwest, I have sometimes taken the wrong path. These unmarked paths seem inviting at first, but before too long they narrow and end, leaving me frustrated and sometimes lost. Over time I have learned, sometimes the hard way, that the only sure way to get to where I want to go is to follow a well-marked path. When I look back on my life, I see many times when I went down the wrong path. Ignoring advice, avoiding friends and trying to do everything my own way, I made some really bad choices. Instead of trying to be the best that I could be, I chose drug abuse. Instead of doing what I needed to do to have the best in life, I became content living with the worst.

Finally, when I had reached rock bottom, a friend who had struggled with similar issues in the past convinced me to visit his church with him. Seeing for myself the effect faith in Christ had on the lives of the people around me, I made the decision to let the Lord's ways guide my life. Since that day I have never looked back, because I see so many good opportunities ahead. I finally learned that God's path is the only path worth walking.

Prayer: *Dear Lord, when we begin to get lost, help us to remember that your way is always open, waiting to lead us to you. Amen*

Thought for the day: With God, I can trust that I'm on the right path.

Mark A. Carter (Oregon, US)

In God's presence

Read Mark 3:13–19

[Jesus] went up the mountain and called to him those whom he wanted… And he appointed twelve, whom he also named apostles, to be with him, and to be sent out to proclaim the message, and to have authority to cast out demons.
Mark 3:13–15 (NRSV)

I have recently been spending more time reading God's word and praying, and though I could be more consistent in my practice, every day I grow closer to God than I was the day before. When I read scripture it becomes God's voice to me, and I learn what he is calling me to do. I pray that as I draw closer to God day by day, I will be better equipped to serve him.

In Mark 3:13–15, Jesus first called the disciples to himself and then sent them out to preach, heal and minister to those in need. In Jesus' presence, they could receive the anointing and the boldness to serve others. I have found that since I've grown closer to God, I am better able to share his word with others. Without first going to him, we won't have much to give to others. Being in God's presence equips us to go out and serve.

Prayer: *Dear Lord, draw us closer to you each day. Help us to hear your voice in your word so that we may share your love with others. In Jesus' name. Amen*

Thought for the day: How can I draw closer to God today?

Enid Adah Nyinomujuni (Dar es Salaam, Tanzania)

Joy and gladness

Read Psalm 104:10–28

'Holy, holy, holy is the Lord Almighty; the whole earth is full of his glory.'
Isaiah 6:3 (NIV)

As I sat at my window watching the rain fall on the leaves, I reflected on how much I had been through since my cancer diagnosis. Five rounds of chemotherapy, a bone marrow transplant and six months in the hospital had left my body, mind and soul exhausted. My world had become grey, dark and lonely. I prayed for something, anything, to lift my spirits.

As the rain hit the leaves, I felt my prayer being answered. The droplets splashed and sparkled in the air, catching bits of light and refracting to make an array of colours. As the wind moved through the trees, the branches danced and swayed; loud cracks of thunder sounded almost like a rhythm. In the world that I thought of as grey and dark, music and colour rivalled even the most beautiful language of today's psalm. I just had to open my eyes to look for it.

Sometimes during our most trying days, we lose our ability to see the beauty that exists around us – in God and in ourselves. While it may not seem true at times, the world is shining with the radiance of our creator. In our most difficult moments, it is more important than ever to see that divine light.

Prayer: *God of all beauty, thank you for the grace and gladness you have woven into the world. Help us to look for your light so that our hearts can be filled with your love. Amen*

Thought for the day: Even in the darkest of storms, joy and gladness exist with God.

Samuel Felderman (Iowa, US)

Love like Jesus

Read John 13:1–15

Having loved his own who were in the world, [Jesus] loved them to the end.

John 13:1 (NIV)

I suspect that all of us have felt let down or disappointed by someone. When this happens, we may be tempted to give up on the person who has made us feel that way. We may feel hurt to the point of despair. But we can choose to maintain peace by turning to God.

Jesus had every reason to give up on his disciples for their inconstancy and their doubts, and he knew of Judas' plot to betray him. And yet Jesus stayed with them, ate with them and astounded them by washing their feet. Jesus repeatedly showed loyalty, humility and love.

We can learn so much by looking at Jesus' actions. Jesus challenged his disciples, and all of us, to follow his example. Thankfully, we have the Holy Spirit to help us serve and love others – even when we feel that they have wronged us.

Prayer: *Dear Lord, strengthen us to love others even when we feel hurt, bitter or disappointed. Help us to demonstrate your grace and forgiveness. Amen*

Thought for the day: How will I follow Jesus' example today?

Lynda J. Samuel (Scotland, United Kingdom)

God's comfort

Read Psalm 4:1–8

In peace I will lie down and sleep, for you alone, Lord, make me dwell in safety.
Psalm 4:8 (NIV)

One Saturday night as my wife and I were babysitting our grandsons, I learned a valuable lesson from God.

After I had read a few bedtime stories to them, it was time for the younger one to go to sleep. He lay peacefully in his cot, so I stealthily crept from the room. Downstairs, as we prepared our three-year-old grandson for bed, I heard the little one cry out in distress. As I entered the room, I found him panting and sobbing, but when he saw me, he calmed down. As I sat with him in a rocking chair, attempting to comfort him, I realised how God, through this child, was comforting me.

At times, we may be like my little grandson. When life doesn't go our way, we can become scared or feel we're at the end of our rope. Our Father God knows how to give perfect love to comfort us in our hopelessness and fear. When we are at our lowest, God wants to surround us with comfort and peace, and whisper those words of Psalm 46:10: 'Be still, and know that I am God.'

Prayer: *God of comfort and peace, help us to trust that you have us in your arms now and forevermore. Amen*

Thought for the day: God can comfort me in any situation.

David Payne (Missouri, US)

Grandma's faith

Read Deuteronomy 6:1–9

Train children in the right way, and when old, they will not stray.
Proverbs 22:6 (NRSV)

When I was growing up, I watched and listened as my grandma read her Bible aloud every night before she went to bed. I wondered why she did it. But watching my grandma practise her faith made me want to know God. I wanted to know what sustained and nourished her through pain and sorrow and gave her sheer joy in living. I wanted to know where my grandma found her strength. As I grew older, I understood that having a connection to her creator gave her hope and got her through life's most difficult times.

Over and over, I return to the image of my grandma reading her Bible. From her example I have learned that God alone gives me strength in my weakness, light in my darkness, comfort in my distress and eternal life in my death. God used my grandma's simple but profound example to help me in my own journey towards him. And as I practise my own faith today, I never know what impact it might have on someone else or how God might use me. Let us all live out our faith so that others can see and hear the love of God.

Prayer: *Dear Lord, thank you for giving us strength through your word. Help us to be witnesses of faith to others every day. Amen*

Thought for the day: How can I be an example of faithful witness to others?

Xavia Arndt Sheffield (Pennsylvania, US)

An invitation from God

Read John 14:12–14
'I will do whatever you ask in my name, so that the Father may be glorified in the Son.'
John 14:13 (NRSV)

At the age of 23 I married a man who was not a Christian. Our lives became extremely busy in running a school. All the time I prayed for my husband's salvation.

One day, after we had been married for 30 years, my husband showed me an invitation he had received to a Christian crusade to be held in Tokyo. Feeling a leading from God, we went.

At the end of the evening, when the leader invited participants to accept Christ, my husband bowed his head before the Lord. He believed in Jesus that day, and at Christmas that year he was baptised. His life was filled with eternal hope, joy and service to God. When a new school building was built, he led a Christian dedication ceremony. When our church was in need of a new place to worship, we offered the all-purpose room at our school – and my husband provided a cross for the platform. He invited the students to Sunday worship.

This is the way in which the Lord answered my many years of prayer. I experienced the grace of the Lord, grace that human wisdom cannot comprehend.

Prayer: *Our loving Father, use us as channels of your love. Be with us and help us to become good witnesses for you. Amen*

Thought for the day: Persistence in prayer is never a waste.

Itsuko Kunori (Gunma Prefecture, Japan)

Desire to serve

Read Psalm 139:1–10
'Before they call I will answer; while they are still speaking I will hear.'
Isaiah 65:24 (NIV)

Moved by the power of the Holy Spirit, I had asked Jesus to be the Lord and Saviour of my life. Soon thereafter, I began learning more from the Bible and Christian writers about the incredible love that God has for me. I have come to see that we are to share with others the love of God through caring words and actions.

One day, I was praying about how I could practise being a Christ-follower through one of the regular ministries at my church. But none of them seemed to fit me, so I put the thought aside. Then, at a Sunday service, our minister announced the church's intention to start a new caring ministry among the lonely and housebound, and asked for volunteers. That invitation was life-changing for me and was the beginning of my years of participation in many different caring ministries.

I sometimes wonder if God was so glad I had finally come to the point of wanting to serve that he just couldn't wait to send the answer to my prayer. Whatever the reason, to God be the glory!

Prayer: *Almighty God, thank you for knowing us so deeply that you bring together our desire to serve you and opportunities to do so. In the name of Jesus, we pray. Amen*

Thought for the day: How will I be open to God's invitation to serve today?

Bob Peterson (Texas, US)

Changes

Read 2 Corinthians 4:7–18

Even if our bodies are breaking down on the outside, the person that we are on the inside is being renewed every day.
2 Corinthians 4:16 (CEB)

I love to walk on the beach looking for seashells. When I was younger, I dreamed of discovering a perfect conch or whelk. In all my days of beachcombing, however, I've seen mostly chipped scallops, common cockles, barnacle-infested mussels and the pieces of once-whole whelks. As I've grown older, I have come to appreciate the small, smooth pieces that roll in with the waves. The purple and cream ones are my favourite, but there are also lovely pinks, browns, blacks and even iridescent golds. Worn by tides and time, they are not the vessels they once were. Instead, they have become beautiful in a new way.

Like those shells, I am not now what I once was. Ageing, illnesses and extensive facial surgery have changed my physical appearance. Yet, because of God's abiding love and guidance, I still have value and beauty. My earthen vessel may not be as young as it once was, but I take comfort in knowing that I am an ever-evolving creation. As today's reading reminds us, 'We have this treasure in clay pots so that the awesome power belongs to God and doesn't come from us' (2 Corinthians 4:7). No matter what our physical changes are, our actions can speak of God's power and renewing presence in our lives.

Prayer: *Dear Father, thank you for abiding with us through life's changes. Help us to become new creations in you so that others can see the power of your love. Amen*

Thought for the day: How can I glorify God in this stage of my life?

Regina K. Carson (Virginia, US)

Faithful servant

Read 1 Samuel 3:1–10

Love the Lord your God with all your heart and with all your soul and with all your strength.
Deuteronomy 6:5 (NIV)

One of my favourite Bible stories is that of Samuel. His mother, Hannah, had begged God to give her a child. God blessed her with a son, Samuel, whom Hannah brought to serve in the temple.

We can imagine little Samuel helping Eli, the high priest in the temple of Shiloh. Samuel might have done chores and run errands for Eli and for the believers who came to the temple. Samuel's work must have been hard, but he served diligently as a loving and faithful steward in God's house.

Samuel served God with all his strength. He didn't complain when he thought Eli was calling him in the middle of the night; he was zealous! For Samuel, no work was menial and every job was important. Because Samuel was faithful in small matters, God entrusted him with big matters. Samuel eventually became one of Israel's greatest prophets.

Loving God with all our strength means volunteering our time, talents, care and resources for God and others. No work is menial or degrading in the service of God – every act of service is holy and pleasing to him. The story of Samuel can inspire us to serve God with all our strength.

Prayer: *Dear God, help us to serve you like Samuel did. Remind us to be zealous in all our work, because every act of service is pleasing to you. Amen*

Thought for the day: Every act of faithful service is sacred.

Wati Mollier (Nagaland, India)

Fetch

Read Psalm 28:6–9
Cast all your anxiety on [God], because he cares for you
1 Peter 5:7 (NRSV)

My dog, Fester, loves the game of fetch. Often when he brings the ball back, though, he will not let go of it, and instead it becomes a game of tug-of-war. I tell Fester that if he wants to play fetch, he has to let go of the ball. This made me think of how, when I go to God in prayer with a problem or need, instead of leaving it with him, I start worrying about it again. Holding on to my problems does me no good either.

When I have trouble letting go, it helps me to delve into the Bible and read God's promises. This reminds me that God has the answer to every problem or challenge I will ever face and that he has promised to be with me no matter what. God is never standing around wondering what to do. It is also helpful to recall his past faithfulness in my life – answered prayers and situations that seemed hopeless but which eventually worked out. From the smallest to the biggest problem, if we let go of our worries and let God handle them, he always comes through.

Prayer: *Dear Lord, help us to cast our cares on you, knowing that when we let you handle them, you always have the best solution to our problems. Amen*

Thought for the day: Whatever today brings, I will let God handle it.

Brenda Brooks (Virginia, US)

A natural symphony

Read Genesis 1:1–25

Let the fields be jubilant, and everything in them; let all the trees of the forest sing for joy.
Psalm 96:12 (NIV)

I enjoy walking my dog in a nearby neighbourhood built around a series of small ponds surrounded by large trees and bushes. Often I listen to music on my portable music player as we walk.

One morning the battery died halfway through the first song. At first I was annoyed. However, I began to listen to the rustling of the trees, the calm splashing of small fountains in the centre of the ponds, the chatter of birds, the quacking of a duck and the occasional melody of a wind chime.

Many distractions and activities fight for our attention, from the technology of smart phones and computer screens to the rush of day-to-day chores and business. Yet none of this can compare to the melodies, art and miracles of God's creation.

I still enjoy walking with my music player. Every now and then, though, I leave it at home and enjoy the beauty of God's creation. When I choose not to let my music block out the world around me, I recognise that God has composed an entire symphony of peaceful sounds. And it is beautiful music, indeed.

Prayer: *Dear God, help us to take the time to enjoy and care for the world you created. Amen*

Thought for the day: I will listen attentively for God's wonders today.

Lisa Tate (New Mexico, US)

A timely gift

Read Matthew 8:23–27

The disciples went and woke [Jesus], saying, 'Lord, save us! We're going to drown!'… Then he got up and rebuked the winds and the waves, and it was completely calm.
Matthew 8:25–26 (NIV)

Until my sister passed away, she would send me *El Aposento Alto*, the Spanish-language edition of *The Upper Room*. Last summer, another sister sent a copy of the magazine to me. Little did I know what a source of blessing and strength it would be at that particular time. On 20 September 2017, María, a Category 4 hurricane, hit Puerto Rico. The 16 hours my family and I spent huddled in our home were terrifying, and we prayed for God's mercy. Words can barely describe the difficulty of the subsequent weeks and months.

However, each morning I reached for *El Aposento Alto* because I knew that in it I would find a message of strength and blessing. God's messages sustained us as we waited in the very long queues to purchase food, water or oil to supply light during the long hours of darkness. Reading *El Aposento Alto* each day was the perfect way to share God's love with my family, especially with my son. He had been in the process of working on his doctoral thesis. Not knowing how the storm's aftermath would affect his studies increased his anxiety. But reading God's word each day renewed our spirits as we began to see our situation slowly improve. We knew we could move forward each day because God was by our side.

Prayer: *Ever-present God, when we call out to you in distress, you hear our prayers. Give us strength to face the hard times. In the name of Jesus Christ, we pray. Amen*

Thought for the day: God's sure refuge is stronger than any storm.

Carmen A. González-Bello (Puerto Rico)

Good morning, Lord

Read Exodus 4:10–12

*This is the confidence we have in approaching God: that if we ask
anything according to his will, he hears us.*
1 John 5:14 (NIV)

Last year our church welcomed a new minister. I was immediately
struck by her approach to the morning prayer. She started by saying,
'Good morning, Lord.' Then she continued her conversation with God.

Her way of praying made me think about prayer in general and how
we as Christians communicate with God. Isn't prayer just a conversation? Is kneeling at our bedside or reciting prayers the only way to
talk to him? I don't think so. We have conversations every day with our
family members, our colleagues and our friends. Maybe God would like
us to think of prayer as that same type of conversation.

I have now started talking to God in a conversational way. I feel
closer and speak more often to him than I would if I only prayed on
my knees morning and night. I can have these prayer conversations as
I drive my car, as I sit in my garden with a cup of tea or as I wake up to
another day that God has given me. Any time can be a good time for a
conversation with him.

Prayer: *Good morning, Lord. I have much to share with you. Thank you
for this time together. Amen*

Thought for the day: Today I will try praying in a new way.

Al Alexander (North Carolina, US)

PRAYER FOCUS: THOSE LEARNING TO PRAY

Learning to trust

Read Matthew 17:14–20

'I know the plans I have for you,' declares the Lord, 'plans to prosper you and not to harm you, plans to give you hope and a future.'
Jeremiah 29:11 (NIV)

Years ago, I spent a great deal of time in the mountains rock-climbing, hiking and camping with friends. At the time I had a beloved dog that often came with me. When the paths required us to squeeze between rocks or climb up or down narrow, steep paths, my dog had to trust me to carry her through safely.

As a young dog, she resisted coming close enough for me to hold her, and after much coaxing would stiffen and twist until I set her feet on easy ground. Once we had safely made our way through, she would wag her tail and shake and snort in relief. As she matured, though, she learned to trust me – then we could manoeuvre through all kinds of places!

I often remember my dog when I encounter problems and sense God encouraging me to be more trusting. Do I resist when God wants to pick me up and pull me through, or do I walk closer and allow him to carry me? As I continue to experience God's trustworthiness, I know I am always secure when I draw near to him.

Prayer: *Faithful and loving God, help us to trust you with everything in life. Amen*

Thought for the day: When troubles arise, I will trust God to carry me through.

Carrie Knight Kitzmiller (Texas, US)

A little sip

Read John 4:7–15

[The Lord] satisfies the thirsty and fills the hungry with good things.
Psalm 107:9 (NIV)

My prayer partner lives in a different area of the country from me. When we lived in the same city, we prayed with each other weekly. Although over the years she has moved to three different places, we continue to pray by phone.

Occasionally we are both busy, so we don't pray together as often. But eventually one of us will text the other to arrange our prayer time. We always spend the first few minutes catching up on our lives, then we ask each other about our prayer requests. Finally, we pray.

During a recent call, we remarked that our time together was like having our thirst quenched. We both laughed when my friend said, 'All we needed was just a little sip.' Psalm 107:9 tells us that God satisfies thirsty souls.

Praying doesn't have to be complicated or follow a certain ritual. It's simply talking to God as a friend, coming to our creator honestly and openly about our cares and concerns. When my friend and I end our prayer time together, we say goodbye knowing that we can both continue our conversation with God.

Prayer: *Dear God, thank you for friends who help us to spend time in your presence and find peace in the power of your love. Amen*

Thought for the day: Prayer connects me to others and to God.

Kathy Gaillard (Wisconsin, US)

Echoes of God's word

Read Acts 2:17–21
'Seek first [God's] kingdom and his righteousness, and all these things will be given to you as well.'
Matthew 6:33 (NIV)

Many years ago our family went on a holiday trip to Europe. One day we went on a sightseeing trip on the famous Königssee near Berchtesgaden in Bavaria, Germany. Königssee is a deep lake surrounded by high mountains that create an enormous echo. The guide on the electric ferry was also a good trumpet player; so as we reached the middle of the lake, the ferry stopped and he played a short piece of music. Seconds after he finished, the music was thrown several times back and forth among the mountains.

This experience has made me think about how the word of God can be like an echo in our hearts and thoughts – not just for seconds but through many years. Today's quoted verse is one of my favourites. Another verse that has become an anchor for me is Acts 2:21: 'Everyone who calls on the name of the Lord will be saved.' These verses and many others have brought me hope for this life and the next. My prayer is that I will allow these verses to speak through me so that they may echo in the lives of those I meet.

Prayer: *Father in heaven, thank you for your word that tells us about your limitless love. Help us to let your love live in our hearts. In the name of Jesus. Amen*

Thought for the day: God's word can live in me and flow through me to others.

Øystein Brinch (Oslo, Norway)

Lasting beauty

Read Isaiah 40:28–31

Charm is deceptive, and beauty is fleeting; but a woman who fears the Lord is to be praised.
Proverbs 31:30 (NIV)

My life has not been the same since my breast cancer diagnosis. When I look in the mirror, I do not like what I see. I feel as if I have aged ten years. My hair is short and receding, thin on the top and speckled with grey. My eyelashes and eyebrows are barely visible. It is difficult to find pretty blouses or dresses during the summer because I have only one breast. I was not prepared for the permanent changes that chemotherapy and a mastectomy have caused.

But throughout this journey, people have been watching me. They weren't looking at my physical changes; they were watching my walk with God. My strength – which comes from God – has been encouraging to others. Though my walk has not been easy, it is comforting to know that my faith is helping others.

Like most people, I want to look appealing – to myself and others. But while circumstances and age have changed my appearance, I am learning to look beyond my physical imperfections. I may look different on the outside, but my desire to please God has not changed. Beauty fades, but my relationship with God will last throughout eternity.

Prayer: *Dear Lord, help us to maintain a strong relationship with you through tough times, for our good and the good of others. Amen*

Thought for the day: Today I will seek to see Christ in myself.

Sherri Pickett (California, US)

'Be opened'

Read Mark 7:31–37

*[Jesus] looked up to heaven and with a deep sigh said to him,
'Ephphatha!' (which means 'Be opened!').*
Mark 7:34 (NIV)

At a recent parish retreat we were asked to share a personal story about a profound experience that taught us something about ourselves. The story I first thought of telling involved a deep healing experience. But certain details connected to my experience were too intimate, so I chose to share a different story. Fear and shame had stopped me. I was worried about what people would think if they learned such intimate details about me.

Then someone else told a story that was similar to the one I had been too afraid to tell. I ended up wishing I'd had the courage to share my original story with the group. Who knows what further healing might have come had I opened up and entered a more vulnerable space as this person had done?

God wants us to move beyond our fear and shame. He wants us to live openly, honestly, into the fullness of who and what we are – who he created us to be. That means entering a space of compassion and vulnerability, in the way that Jesus did. Often, it is in those moments of raw, unabashed honesty that God speaks and moves through us most powerfully.

Prayer: *O God, help us to open up our lives to others who want what is best for us. In the name of Jesus, we pray. Amen*

Thought for the day: God calls me to share my story with honesty and courage.

Jennifer A. Hudson (Connecticut, US)

No unimportant part

Read 1 Corinthians 12:12–31

The parts of the body that people think are the weakest are the most necessary.
1 Corinthians 12:22 (CEB)

I recently joined a church choir. At my age I can no longer hit the high notes, so I've switched from singing soprano to the lower range of alto.

At first, I envied the sopranos, who often carry the melody. Their clear, high notes are the most noticed sounds in our choir. How impressive it is when they hit a high G! Meanwhile, I sing the more subtle alto tones that I hardly used to notice.

I changed my perspective, however, while listening to a recording of our latest performance. I realised that every vocalist has an important part in a choir. While the altos don't normally carry the melody, our voices add an exquisite harmony that enhances the choir's performance.

Like altos, many church members perform roles that seem to fade into the background. Some collect donations for projects. Others serve on committees that plan special events. Some work in the kitchen, preparing meals. Still others ensure that the garden is tended. No matter how minor they may seem, all these jobs are important to the life of the church.

Whatever talents we have, we can use them not to receive applause but to focus on doing our part in serving God.

Prayer: *God of all voices, help us to perform our part of the work to the best of our ability, knowing that we are serving you. Amen*

Thought for the day: My role is important to the church.

Lu Fullilove (Texas, US)

Hope for the world

Read 1 John 5:1–5
Who is it that overcomes the world? Only the one who believes that Jesus is the Son of God.
1 John 5:5 (NIV)

On 28 September 2018, a 7.5 magnitude earthquake hit the Indonesian island of Sulawesi, triggering tsunami waves of nearly six metres and inflicting a death toll of more than 2,000. Many more people were missing. I cried, 'Oh, God, how many more disasters?' Each time people perish in a natural disaster, I feel pain for this world.

As I was feeling depressed by the aftermath of the earthquake in Sulawesi, I attended a Sunday service at my home church. The preacher for the day read some of today's reading from 1 John, which says that we shall 'overcome the world' if we keep our faith, believing in our Lord Jesus Christ's victory. Relief came upon me with hope that Jesus will rescue us. 'The sound of weeping and of crying will be heard… no more' (Isaiah 65:19). 'There will be no more death or mourning or crying or pain' (Revelation 21:4). These words calm me and bring me peace.

The world is suffering, but we have hope for the future when we trust God and believe in the Lord Jesus Christ.

Prayer: *Dear God, comfort us in our present suffering and pain. Help us to have faith in a future with you. In Jesus' name, we pray. Amen*

Thought for the day: God's words can comfort me through suffering.

Kong Peng Sun (Singapore)

A sacred pause

Read Luke 5:12–16

'Come to me, all you who are weary and burdened, and I will give you rest.'
Matthew 11:28 (NIV)

When my children were young, I taught them at home. Lunchtime was usually my first break of the day. At noon, I gathered everyone to eat, and we held hands to pray. But as I bowed my head and spoke thankful words to God, my mind sprinted ahead: 'Eat quickly, put away the dishes, get ready for the afternoon's lessons, begin dinner preparations…'

On one especially hectic day, before I prayed I consciously took a slow, deep breath. I relaxed my shoulders. I cleared my head. I prepared my heart to be thankful to God for our food, my children and all the good in my life. It was a sacred pause to recognise my shortcomings and God's ability to provide. My needs were many in the middle of a busy day – not only food, but also energy, patience and discipline. Most of all, I needed a moment of God's peace before I started my afternoon.

God meets us where we are: overburdened, tired, running on empty. Not only is God the provider of the gift of food at mealtimes, but he is also the giver of renewed energy, contentment and balance for the hours ahead. By quietly entering into God's presence, we offer a moment of gratitude and receive the peace that he promises.

Prayer: *Father God, remind us to pause and enter into your presence many times each day. As we offer our gratitude, may we receive the rest and peace you promise. Amen*

Thought for the day: I can enter into God's presence any time of day.

Natalie D. Hall (Texas, US)

Signs

Read Matthew 4:18–22
Trust in the Lord with all your heart and lean not on your own understanding.
Proverbs 3:5 (NIV)

On a beautiful autumn day, I drove along a narrow, curving road on a mountain in North Carolina. As I began the descent, multiple temporary road signs warned me that the road ahead was deteriorating and becoming dangerous. I gripped the steering wheel, tapped the brakes and prepared for the worst. But the next several miles did not get narrower or curvier. In fact, the road hardly changed at all. At the foot of the mountain, I thought, 'Those signs ruined my drive!'

Then I thought about the ominous 'signs' I place in my own path – like the one that whines 'Day Worsens After Lunch' or the one that warns 'Life Worsens After 60'. Those signs ruin my day and invite fear into my life.

I don't need those signs anyway – Jesus has given me the guidance I need. Just as the disciples dropped their nets and followed Jesus, I must drop my 'signs' and follow him. With Jesus by my side, I can ascend the mountain of my fear and move forward despite obstacles. And with confidence in Jesus' love, I can find joy in my life's journey.

Prayer: *Dear God, help us to trust in you and rejoice in the journeys of our lives. Help us to let go of negative thoughts so that we can follow you. Amen*

Thought for the day: What 'signs' keep me from following Christ?

K. Anne Smith (Tennessee, US)

Changed

Read 2 Corinthians 5:16–21

If anyone is in Christ, the new creation has come: the old has gone, the new is here!
2 Corinthians 5:17 (NIV)

When I became a Christian, I noticed many positive changes in my life. I became more joyful and peaceful. I started going to church, and I enjoyed having fellowship with other believers. Previously the Bible had seemed like any other book, but I started to love reading scripture, which had become alive to me. God became real and personal. I had truly become a new creation in Christ: old things had passed away, and all things had become new. Even my older brother noticed the changes and commented, 'Surely there is such a thing as salvation. This girl has changed.'

As the years pass by, I continue to change as I grow in my faith and knowledge of Jesus Christ. People change as they grow and experience new things. But God, the creator of all things, is dependable and trustworthy. What a blessing to know that God's love for us never changes.

Prayer: *Dear God, thank you for your steadfast love. Help us to continually change into the likeness of Jesus. As Jesus taught us, we pray, 'Our Father in heaven, hallowed be your name, your kingdom come, your will be done, on earth as it is in heaven. Give us today our daily bread. And forgive us our debts, as we also have forgiven our debtors. And lead us not into temptation, but deliver us from the evil one.'* Amen*

Thought for the day: How has following Christ transformed me?

Charity M. Kiregyera (Kampala, Uganda)

PRAYER FOCUS: THOSE WHO HAVE NOT HEARD THE GOSPEL
*Matthew 6:9–13

Overcoming sin

Read Romans 8:5–14

If you live according to the flesh, you will die; but if by the Spirit you put to death the misdeeds of the body, you will live.
Romans 8:13 (NIV)

Late one evening, I saw a large spider crawling in my bathroom. Thankfully, this didn't send me into a horrified yelling fit. The spider's presence did, however, motivate me to remove it – fast.

Soon after getting rid of the spider, I thought of my reaction to my sin. God spoke clearly to my heart: 'If you were that quick and serious about eliminating sin from your life, think how many fewer problems you would have and how much better your life would be.'

As we see in the scripture verse quoted above, God's word gives us firm counsel about the importance of getting rid of our sin. If we are determined and disciplined, we can overcome our sin through confession, repentance and the power of the Holy Spirit, trusting that God is always ready to forgive us.

Prayer: *Dear Lord, thank you for the gifts of Jesus Christ, your Holy Spirit and your word – all of which empower us to overcome sin. In Jesus' name. Amen*

Thought for the day: With God's help, I can overcome my sin.

Tyler Myers (Ohio, US)

Unseen

Read 1 Samuel 16:1–13

The Lord said to Samuel, 'Do not consider his appearance or his height, for I have rejected him. The Lord does not look at the things people look at. People look at the outward appearance, but the Lord looks at the heart.'
1 Samuel 16:7 (NIV)

One day while I was pruning a tree outside my house, a woman came up to me and asked why I was doing it. I told her that the leaves and branches were being eaten by caterpillars and weren't growing, so I was cutting them to allow new shoots to grow. This morning while I was watering my plants, she came again and asked, 'Why are the leaves not growing? You should not have cut the leaves and branches!' I told her that a new leaf was growing – it was just small. She looked at the branch and said, 'I don't see it!' Then she walked away.

I can sometimes be like that woman – only seeing what is in plain sight, not looking deeper to what is hidden. When suffering comes, I may only notice the suffering and not what God provides during hardship. I may longingly compare my life to others' instead of appreciating the blessings God has given me.

Today's scripture reading tells us that God sees deeper, beyond the outward appearance. When God is present in my life, he helps me to look for what lies hidden. By staying close to him, I can experience his unseen guidance and peace in any situation.

Prayer: *Dear God, help us to look for what lies hidden. Draw us close to you, and guide us with your compassionate heart. Amen*

Thought for the day: With God's help, I can see beyond what is in plain sight.

Linda Chandra (Banten, Indonesia)

Table fellowship

Read Ephesians 4:3–6

[Those who accepted Peter's message and were baptised] devoted themselves to the apostles' teaching and to fellowship, to the breaking of bread and to prayer.
Acts 2:42 (NIV)

Every day when Edwin, my Nigerian college roommate, would prepare his native foods in our kitchen, the house would fill with a distinct aroma that didn't appeal to my American palate. One afternoon, Edwin invited me to share his evening meal. Finding no suitable excuse, I reluctantly agreed. We sat across from each other at the table, where Edwin had placed one pot of a soup-like mixture and one plate that held a ball of biscuit dough. After the blessing Edwin explained, 'In my country, we eat from one bowl as a sign of friendship.' He took a piece of dough, dipped it in the soup and ate the two together. I was humbled that Edwin counted me as a friend, and this meal became sacred to me. It reminded me of Holy Communion – one loaf, one cup, one body, one people. Better than ever before, I understood that transformation happens at the Lord's table. God unites people into the body of Christ.

This same transformation happens when we sit down to share a meal at church, eat with people who are experiencing homelessness or gather for Holy Communion. Jesus is with us in the breaking of bread. We have the opportunity to invite others to share this meal, and around the Lord's table, we will be united as God's family.

Prayer: *Dear Lord Jesus, as you invited us to the table and into your family, help us invite others to your table and into your family. Amen*

Thought for the day: At the table, I unite with other Christians as my family.

Kevin Thomas (Alabama, US)

Comfort in loneliness

Read Psalm 147:1–7

[God] hath said, I will never leave thee, nor forsake thee.
Hebrews 13:5 (KJV)

I work in a care home with residents who have middle-to-late-stage dementia. One day, a resident named Margaret told me that she felt lonely and didn't know where her family was. She didn't remember that her family had recently visited. I tried to reassure her that she was not alone, and I gave her a hug and a smile. But it seemed as though that wasn't what she needed to hear in that moment. Margaret started to walk away and then turned around to look at me. She said, 'God said he will never leave us or forsake us.' I told her that she was absolutely right. As she walked away, she seemed to feel better. Although Margaret struggled to remember many things, she remembered a Bible verse that brought her comfort at the right time.

I believe that God sends us the encouragement we need in the exact moment we need it – through songs, experiences, other people and the Bible. I have experienced this in my own life and witnessed it in the lives of others. We serve a mighty God! Whatever we're facing today, we can trust that God is there for us. He will never leave us or forsake us, and we are never alone.

Prayer: *Dear Lord, guide us to show your love to those who are lonely. During our own times of loneliness, remind us that you are with us. Amen*

Thought for the day: Scripture serves as my reminder that God is always with me.

Jenny McBride (Alabama, US)

A beautiful message

Read Isaiah 58:7–11

A generous person will prosper; whoever refreshes others will be refreshed.
Proverbs 11:25 (NIV)

Every time my family visits the northern part of Puerto Rico, I suggest going to the city where I was born. One year, our visit coincided with a craft fair in the market square. Artisans and vendors displayed an array of merchandise. Music filled the air as musicians entertained the crowds. It was a festive and joyful day with much to see and do.

During the busiest time of the day, my daughter queued to buy lunch at a food stall. It was hot, and people complained about the heat and the long queue. Suddenly a dishevelled woman approached. She seemed disoriented, speaking unintelligibly, and a few customers shied away from her. But the owner of the food stall immediately stopped what he was doing and approached the woman in a gentle manner. His voice was filled with compassion when he asked if she would like something to eat. He quickly served her a generous meal. Moments later, she was smiling as she went on her way.

My daughter returned to us with tears in her eyes. She said, 'I have witnessed and heard the most beautiful message. It has opened my eyes and helped change my attitude. I pray I can honour God by showing mercy and compassion to others.'

Prayer: *O God, help us to abide in your love and to show compassion to others, just as Jesus taught us. Amen*

Thought for the day: God rejoices in my acts of kindness.

María M. Urdaz (Puerto Rico)

Where the big fish live

Read James 1:1–12

Blessed is the one who perseveres under trial because, having stood the test, that person will receive the crown of life that the Lord has promised to those who love him.

James 1:12 (NIV)

I recently took my eight-year-old grandson fishing for the first time. We spent much of the day casting our lines into the middle of the lake. He was excited to catch and release some small fish, but he really wanted to catch a much bigger one. As the day wore on, he suggested we cast into the shadows where the water was full of reeds. I told him it would be risky, and that we would probably get our hooks tangled up. 'But Grandpa,' he said, 'I think that's where the big fish live.' So we cast into the shadows, and our lines got tangled with the reeds more than once. But we persevered and finally knew the thrill of hooking a big fish.

Jesus did not promise us that following him would be easy. It may seem safer to keep to our usual routines rather than to take a risk by speaking about and acting on our faith. But James tells us that if we faithfully persevere, the Lord promises us a great reward.

Prayer: *Gracious and loving God, thank you for the wisdom of children. Give us courage to take a risk and to persevere for the sake of Christ. In Jesus' name, we pray. Amen*

Thought for the day: Following Christ can be risky, but it's always worth it.

Doug Wingert (Arizona, US)

Alive and active

Read Hebrews 4:12–16
The word of God is alive and active.
Hebrews 4:12 (NIV)

I made yoghurt from scratch the other day and was amazed at how simple the process was. All I had to do was bring milk to a rolling boil and then lower the temperature. When the liquid was cool enough, I dropped in a dollop of yoghurt that contained active live cultures. Then I covered the whole thing and let it sit for 24 hours. During that time, the cultures multiplied and grew, turning the whole bowl of milk into beautiful creamy yoghurt. The active cultures were real, even though I couldn't see them.

The day after I made the yoghurt, I was sitting in church listening to my minister talking about the word of God being alive and active. I couldn't help but think of the yoghurt.

I wonder if a little of God's truth added to my life could grow and create change until it affects my whole being. I wonder how much God's word is changing me without my noticing. And how much change will continue to happen if I add more scripture to my heart, day after day? The possibilities fill me with excitement and hope!

Prayer: *Thank you, Lord, that your word is alive and can create change in us so that we become more obedient to you. Amen*

Thought for the day: The word of God creates change in my heart.

Cara Grandle (Oregon, US)

Wind and wave

Read Mark 4:35–41

'Who is this? Even the wind and the waves obey him!'
Mark 4:41 (NIV)

Anyone who has travelled with me knows that I can fall asleep in uncomfortable and unconventional places. Whether on crowded buses or on busy trains – sitting or standing – I'll find a way to get some shut-eye. However, I can't say that a small fishing boat in the midst of one of Galilee's squalls would be my idea of a pleasant place for a nap. But it seemed to be adequate for Jesus. While his disciples battened down the boat against the raging sea, Jesus settled down for a snooze.

Often we cry out as the disciples did: 'Save me, Lord! Don't you even care?' After Jesus had rebuked the wind and the disciples, they were awestruck: 'Who is this? Even the wind and the waves obey him!' We must ask ourselves: 'Who is God, in whom I claim to trust? Do I rest in the arms of a creator and sustainer, or have I constructed a cold and distant saviour who is powerless to meet my needs?'

While we might fear for our lives in the storm, God remains unthreatened. If we choose to focus on the storm, it will inevitably overtake us. But if we choose to focus on God's presence and power, we can be confident that our circumstances hold no power against the master of wind and wave.

Prayer: *Lord God, teach us to seek you during the storms of life. Give us faith to trust in your everlasting love for us. Amen*

Thought for the day: Today I will focus on God's power instead of the storm.

Joel Broberg (Minnesota, US)

God of restoration

Read Isaiah 61:1–7

There is a time for everything, and a season for every activity under the heavens.
Ecclesiastes 3:1 (NIV)

One morning, I was looking at new growth on a stem of my potted plant. A few days earlier, the very same stem had looked too old and worn out to produce any new leaves, and I had considered pruning it. But in that short time, the plant produced new green leaves – not just one, but a cluster of three!

Sometimes I feel the way my plant looked. We may feel so worn out that we think we can't do anything. But God can restore and make everything new. He is able to bring a harvest even from a field that seems barren to us. There is a purpose and a correct timing for everything under heaven. God has blessings in store for us, if we will be still, believe and receive them.

Prayer: *Dear Lord, we cast all our cares on you, trusting that you can handle every situation better than we can. Amen*

Thought for the day: God is able to restore even the most worn-out parts of me.

Deepika Emmanuel Sagar (Rajasthan, India)

Touchstones

Read Luke 12:22–28

'Who of you by worrying can add a single hour to your life?'
Luke 12:25 (NIV)

During the 25 years I have been reading *The Upper Room*, I've noticed that common themes and favourite passages of scripture seem to return again and again. This passage from Luke 12 may be one of these favourites. At first I thought that over-reliance on certain passages was a problem; other parts of the Bible could be neglected in the process. Then I realised that we all have 'touchstone' passages of scripture because they speak to us in ways that are unique but also universal.

Today the passage from Luke is about the stress and worry for the future that many of us face. But the passage assures us that such concerns are minimal in the grand scheme of things. We leave the passage with peace, resolve and a renewed faith that God will provide for us. This becomes a core message that Christians can share with others, because learning to trust God's provision is one of the most universal facets of the human experience.

Prayer: *Loving God, help us to see the big picture in a world where our daily lives seem consumed with minutiae. Guide us to prioritise what truly matters – our love for you and our neighbour. Amen*

Thought for the day: Despite my worries, I can trust God's provision.

Andrew Billings (Alabama, US)

Confidence to witness

Read Matthew 11:1–11
'Truly I tell you, among those born of women there has not risen anyone greater than John the Baptist; yet whoever is least in the kingdom of heaven is greater than he.'
Matthew 11:11 (NIV)

When I tried to share Jesus with someone who was more successful and more educated than I was, the words tumbled out of my mouth in a confused heap. Then when the person disagreed with me, my mind went blank. I couldn't come up with a quick response. So I walked away, red-faced with embarrassment. 'I'm just not smart enough to tell people about Jesus,' I thought.

One morning, Jesus' words in the verse quoted above challenged my assumption of not being good enough. In them, I heard a personal message that being a member of God's kingdom gives me great value. I had fallen into the trap of measuring my worth by using standards that were not God's standards – education, worldly success and wealth. Those false values kept me feeling inadequate and afraid to talk to others about Jesus.

We each have value because of who Jesus is and what he did for us. And that can't be taken away. When we remember that Jesus is the basis for our self-worth, we can be confident in telling anyone – no matter how rich, successful or educated – about him.

Prayer: *Heavenly Father, may your love and the knowledge that our value is from Christ Jesus help us to share the gospel boldly with others. Amen*

Thought for the day: Because Jesus died for me, I can live boldly for him.

Darlene J. Ellis (Oregon, US)

Waiting

Read Habakkuk 1:1–5

I will take my post… I will keep watch to see what the Lord says to me and how he will respond to my complaint.
Habakkuk 2:1 (CEB)

Few things can dampen our resolve or put our faith to the test more than waiting. While we may struggle to accept it, God's timing is his own. Habakkuk began his dialogue with God with a complaint. In his lament, he demanded God's attention. He pleaded for justice as he looked at the violence and injustice around him in Judah. How could God allow such evil? But judgement against Judah would come. More astounding, the agent of God's judgement would be a people Habakkuk thought of as even more wicked than the people of Judah.

When we question God, we may not expect a response; but Habakkuk did. When he questioned God, he did not quite understand God's plan but vowed to wait. Scripture does not indicate how long the prophet prayed and waited for God's vision, but Habakkuk remained steadfast and waited for God's reply. Habakkuk's prayerful response confirms his faith and obedience to God: 'I will rejoice in the Lord; I will exult in the God of my salvation' (3:18, NRSV). Habakkuk shows us the value of waiting resolutely for God's response, who works for our good.

Prayer: *Everlasting God, thank you for hearing our complaints. Grant us patience as we wait for your response. Amen*

Thought for the day: I will wait on God's promises.

Hazael Alvarado Hernández (Mexico City, Mexico)

With our hearts

Read Matthew 13:18–23

'As for what was sown on good soil, this is the one who hears the word and understands it, who indeed bears fruit and yields.'
Matthew 13:23 (NRSV)

My husband was a brilliant physician who had to retire early because he has Parkinson's disease. Since his voice has become soft and mono-tone, I sometimes have trouble understanding what he is saying. However, our adult son always understands him. One day I asked my husband what was different between our son's approach and mine. He said, 'Our son listens with his heart.' Then I realised that I was so preoccupied with household duties that I was not listening intently enough to hear and understand my husband – his words fell on rocky ground. Our son listened intently with a joyful heart and was able to understand his father.

I began to wonder if this is also the way I approach scripture. Sometimes when I read the Bible, I can be so preoccupied with my to-do list that I don't listen for God's message. Just as I can better understand my husband when I focus on him, I will be better able to hear the message God is sending me if I focus on his word. If we focus and listen with our hearts, we will all be better able to reflect God's love and bear fruit.

Prayer: *Dear God, give us receptive hearts to listen to the needs of others and to hear the message you are giving us through scripture. Amen*

Thought for the day: When I focus on God, I can better understand his message for me.

Karen M. Fite (Alabama, US)

God's hands and feet

Read Luke 10:25–37
'Go and do likewise.'
Luke 10:37 (NIV)

An image of Jesus laughing hangs on a wall in my office. When a friend saw the image of Jesus with his head thrown back and mouth wide open in uproarious laughter, she responded with sadness: 'I don't see how God can laugh with so much suffering in the world.'

I agreed. For many years my communication with God included my doubts as to who he is. One day while watching the news on TV, I saw a pitiful scene of a woman clutching an infant who was starving to death. I lamented, 'God, if you are a loving, compassionate being, how can you allow this?' Suddenly a mental image of a tearful God cradling the mother and child looked at me and said, 'If you are my disciple, how can you allow this?' The question hit me hard. My indignation turned to discomfort. No longer could I indulge in my smug accusations of God. I am responsible.

Since that day, I have begun to pray in a new way. Instead of complaining to God, I now seek insight to discover my role in the face of suffering. That image of Jesus laughing has become not only about humour but also about liberation and understanding my role in God's world.

Prayer: *Dear Lord, open our hearts and minds to see those who are suffering. Give us the courage and tools we need to respond. Amen*

Thought for the day: As God's disciple, I am tasked to care for those in need.

Bill Roy (Florida, US)

A leap of faith

Read Hebrews 11:1–29
Faith is the substance of things hoped for, the evidence of things not seen.
Hebrews 11:1 (KJV)

Recently I visited an art display entitled 'A Leap of Faith'. It featured a pitch-black staircase which would light up only after someone had the courage to mount the first step.

This artwork reminds me of taking that first step with God even when we do not see the whole staircase, trusting that it will lead us to our desired destination. Often we underestimate the importance of every step we take in paving the way to a complete and fulfilling Christian journey.

Hebrews 11 describes how people such as Abraham, Moses and Rahab took that leap of faith. We, too, can grow stronger from difficult situations by stepping into them in faith rather than running away from them. As a result we gain experience that will help us to navigate better as we draw closer to God.

Prayer: *Dear God, give us the courage in difficult situations to take that leap of faith in Jesus as we pray, 'Our Father which art in heaven, Hallowed be thy name. Thy kingdom come, Thy will be done in earth, as it is in heaven. Give us this day our daily bread. And forgive us our debts, as we forgive our debtors. And lead us not into temptation, but deliver us from evil: For thine is the kingdom, and the power, and the glory, forever.'* Amen*

Thought for the day: When I take a leap of faith, my joy in the Lord increases.

Ho Pei Fah (Singapore)

*Matthew 6:9–13

Walk slowly

Read Psalm 1:1–3

*'Be still, and know that I am God! I am exalted among the nations,
I am exalted in the earth.'*
Psalm 46:10 (NRSV)

For many years I regularly drove past a wood alongside the road. To me it was just an unremarkable group of trees. Then one day, traffic was at a standstill. I looked at the trees and noticed a walking path, so a few days later I went back and had a walk through the trees. I saw many varieties of trees and ferns, as well as squirrels and birds. When I looked up, I saw beautiful rays of sun shining through the canopy of leaves. It was tranquil and stunning. When I took the time to walk slowly through the wood, I saw so much more.

Too often in our spiritual lives, we zip through our daily reading of the Bible and close the cover – done for the day. But when we slowly walk through each verse, noticing the words and what they mean in that passage, we will see things that we never noticed before: the struggles of a particular character, the resolution of familiar events and how God is sovereign over it all. We may understand for the first time how a passage fits perfectly with the rest of the chapter ultimately to create a complete book. When we slow down to see that there is so much more, we will find assurance and beauty. The stories of our faith are stunning!

Prayer: *Creator God, may we never be too busy to be amazed by all that is in your world and in your word. Amen*

Thought for the day: Today I will take time to notice the details of God's world.

Bob LaForge (New Jersey, US)

A true friend

Read Philippians 4:4–9

Do not be anxious about anything, but in every situation, by prayer and petition, with thanksgiving, present your requests to God.
Philippians 4:6 (NIV)

For the past two summers I have worked at a Christian holiday camp for young people. The first year made me stronger in my faith and happy to show others the light of Christ working through me. I thought the next year would be the same, but it turned out to be quite the opposite, because I had to deal with bullying from some of the older campers. It was hard to show the light of Christ when hurtful words led me to believe I wasn't good enough. I kept asking myself, 'Why do they treat me like this?' and 'What am I doing wrong?'

Thankfully I had a friend who prayed for me and let me know that all the bullies' negative comments about me were not true. My friend reminded me that my identity comes from Christ. Then I read Philippians 4:6. After reading that verse, I started sharing my troubles with God, asking him to take my burden and give me peace.

I still had to endure the bullying, but I knew that what they said wasn't what Christ thought of me. And I still had a friend who stood alongside me. I held on to God, who led me through it all and helped me to grow. Now I know how much love and peace God provides.

Prayer: *Thank you, God, for helping us learn from our trials. Give us your peace and joy in the midst of them. Amen*

Thought for the day: When I am torn down, God lifts me up.

Kate Reisenauer (South Dakota, US)

Shine your light

Read Matthew 5:13–16

'Let your light shine before others, that they may see your good deeds and glorify your Father in heaven.'
Matthew 5:16 (NIV)

One bleak, cloudy, autumn day, I went to do my grocery shopping. As I approached the shopping centre, I was astounded by an avenue of trees in the full glory of their autumn colours. Against the grey day and grey buildings, the trees stood out with their bright gold and red leaves. They seemed to light up the world around them with their beauty.

I remembered how Jesus said that we as Christians should be the light of the world and thought, 'If only I could light up the world as well as those trees do! How can I do this? Where shall I start?' Pondering these questions, I realised that I needed God's help – I needed to draw closer to him by reading my Bible daily and praying for guidance. As I try to follow the teachings of Jesus more closely, I pray that my light will shine more brightly and point others to God.

Prayer: *Loving God, may our lives show others that we belong to you. Help us to shine brightly to the world around us. Amen*

Thought for the day: Daily opportunities to shine Christ's love abound.

Margaret Martin (Australian Capital Territory, Australia)

The cheering crowd

Read Hebrews 12:1–3

Therefore, since we are surrounded by such a great cloud of witnesses, let us throw off everything that hinders and the sin that so easily entangles.
Hebrews 12:1 (NIV)

I was standing with my hands raised above my head as I gasped for air. My legs and lungs burned from my first cross-country race of the season. I congratulated the person who finished in front of me and continued to cheer on the people still coming in.

After a few minutes it seemed that everyone had finished the race. But the clock was still running, so many people were waiting eagerly for the last runner. Soon a boy came around the corner. A crowd ran beside him, yelling and cheering him on to finish the race. The boy was ecstatic as he crossed the finish line.

As I reflected on this day, I understood Hebrews 12 in a new way. It says that everyone is running the race of life and being encouraged by a huge crowd in heaven and by those around us. When the race is long or we are running uphill, we may think, 'There is no way I can make it.' But God and our supporters cheer, 'You can do it!' Before we know it, we can look back and see all the distance we have covered with the help of our 'cloud of witnesses'.

Prayer: *Dear God, thank you for cheering us on and helping us through hard times. Amen*

Thought for the day: Whom is God calling me to encourage today?

Chris Hemstock (South Dakota, US)

PRAYER FOCUS: LONG-DISTANCE RUNNERS   57

Praying instead

Read Luke 18:1–7

'Can any one of you by worrying add a single hour to your life?'
Matthew 6:27 (NIV)

I used to worry a lot, which produced feelings of fear, sadness or confusion. So I decided to try to turn each worry into a prayer.

Sometimes a scripture verse came to mind when I prayed. When worried about something in the future, I prayed, 'Therefore do not worry about tomorrow… Each day has enough trouble of its own' (Matthew 6:34). When I worried about a loved one, 1 John 5:14 helped me: 'This is the confidence we have in approaching God: that if we ask anything according to his will, he hears us.' When worried and confused about what to do, I remembered, 'If any of you lacks wisdom, you should ask God, who gives generously to all without finding fault, and it will be given to you' (James 1:5). Often, praying the scripture verse resulted in peace.

When no verse came to mind, like the woman in today's reading who repeatedly appealed to the judge, I prayed about the same thing again and again.

Prayer can help keep our worries from resurfacing. If we practise, praying when we are worried can become a habit. Then, over time, our worried thoughts and negative feelings may decrease as God's peace increases.

Prayer: *Loving God, forgive us when we worry. Help us to trust that you can handle all our fears. Amen*

Thought for the day: Praying scripture can bring me peace.

Deb Vellines (Missouri, US)

A helping hand

Read Psalm 41:1–3
Whoever oppresses the poor shows contempt for their Maker, but whoever is kind to the needy honours God.
Proverbs 14:31 (NIV)

I was in a hurry when I came to a stop at a traffic light. A homeless person approached my car. As he came towards the driver's side, I began to assume the worst of him even though he had given me no reason to. I thought about not rolling down the window, but when he looked directly at me, his smile changed my way of thinking. I saw Christ in his smile. He seemed sincere as we talked briefly. Courteously he asked, 'Sir, can you help me?' I felt great empathy for him.

I asked myself what Jesus would do in a similar situation. It was a cold December morning; perhaps the man had not even had a simple cup of coffee. I extended my hand and offered a donation of money. He said: 'Thank you so much, sir, for your love. God bless you a thousand times over, and your family as well.' The traffic light changed and so did my attitude. My encounter with this man reminded me that God shows us abundant compassion every day. We can do no less.

Prayer: *Merciful God, free us from prejudices that keep us from being generous and loving. Help us to see a reflection of Jesus in the faces of those we encounter today and to extend a helping hand to those in need. Amen*

Thought for the day: I can overcome my prejudice when I remember Jesus' love.

Elí Samuel Morales Morales (Puerto Rico)

PRAYER FOCUS: THE HOMELESS

Strength

Read Psalm 27:1–5

The Lord is my light and my salvation; whom shall I fear? the Lord is the strength of my life; of whom shall I be afraid?
Psalm 27:1 (KJV)

My life was going well, but then everything changed. On a visit to the eye clinic I was told I had macular degeneration. 'Wasn't my severe glaucoma enough?' I thought. Then I experienced a meniscus tear and a painful cyst in my knee. 'Wasn't one or the other enough?' Later the same week my doctor informed me that I was a diabetic. 'Lord,' I prayed, 'when is my trouble going to stop?'

I realised I was feeling sorry for myself and questioning God, so I asked him for help. The next moment, I thought of Job. Job's trust in God was amazing, especially considering all he lost and all he went through. Then my thoughts turned to Paul. I thought about all the times he was jailed, whipped and shipwrecked. I wondered how often Job and Paul wondered when their troubles would stop. Then I thought of Jesus' suffering. Jesus was beaten and humiliated, but that wasn't all. Jesus died on a cross, and God offered us salvation.

I believe that God gave me these thoughts to help me to realise that I could endure my problems. I knew that he would love and be with me through everything. I felt better. I felt stronger. God gave me strength then, and he will give me strength tomorrow.

Prayer: *Dear Lord, thank you for your strength that helps us to keep going through pain and change. Amen*

Thought for the day: God's mercies and strength are new every morning.

Margaret Bishop (Kentucky, US)

Small ministry?

Read 1 Corinthians 15:50–58
Always give yourselves fully to the work of the Lord, because you know that your labour in the Lord is not in vain.
1 Corinthians 15:58 (NIV)

My mother's ministry was sending birthday cards with encouraging words. For more than 30 years she sent cards to people and never tired of her work. On the day she died, she had ten birthday cards ready to be posted. When I arrived to help prepare for her funeral, my dad asked me what we should do with the cards. I told him that we needed to post them.

In the week leading up to my mother's funeral, many people told me how much receiving a birthday card from my mother had meant to them. At the funeral, I asked how many people had received a birthday card from my mother. Nearly everyone raised their hand. Mum's ministry seemed like a small thing, but it touched so many lives. She stood firm and let nothing move her as she did the work of the Lord.

We can all strive to accomplish the good that we have the opportunity to do. When we ask God to give us opportunities to serve, we need not worry about the size of our ministry or its outcomes. God will work through us to provide meaningful results, whether we see them in our lifetime or not.

Prayer: *Dear God, thank you for giving us opportunities to serve you by serving others. Amen*

Thought for the day: What ministry is God calling me to today?

Steve Wakefield (Georgia, US)

No limit

Read Psalm 46:1–7
God is our refuge and strength, an ever-present help in trouble.
Psalm 46:1 (NIV)

A gospel singer in my country wrote a song with the words, 'Go upward, forward. There is no limit.' When I heard this song, I was working in the daytime and leading a Bible study twice a month in the evening. I was often surrounded by worries about daily life and the future, and these worries clouded my ability to connect with and reflect on God. But through the song I felt that God was speaking directly to my heart, saying, 'Don't be discouraged. Just move forward. I am always with you and will provide for you.' I was filled with relief and peace. I was able to face my challenges instead of running away, even though my situation had not changed.

During my difficult time, God used a gospel singer's gift to connect with and encourage me. Each day we can use the gifts God has given us to move upward, press forward and hopefully encourage others along the way. With God, there truly is no limit.

Prayer: *Gracious God, thank you for being faithful to your promises. Encourage us to move forward each day. Amen*

Thought for the day: I bless others by embracing the gifts God has given me.

Eiko Kato (Miyagi Prefecture, Japan)

Freedom

Read John 8:34–38
'If the Son sets you free, you will be free indeed.'
John 8:36 (NIV)

I am in prison, but I am freer now than I was prior to incarceration. Though I was a minister, worship leader and staff member in several congregations, I lost touch with the God I shared with others. Through a pattern of poor choices and the desire to be seen as successful, I lived a double life that came crashing down and hurt many people. Because I never slowed down or paused to listen to God, I became oblivious to my own sin.

I now realise that I had built my life around my own desires and not on the solid foundation of Christ. While I have been in prison, my parents have died, my children have been adopted and my wife and I are finalising our divorce. In the last few years, the life I built has been torn down. It has been painful, but sometimes we have to let go of what we hold dear and cling to God instead. Jesus said, 'Come with me… to a quiet place' (Mark 6:31). I never imagined that for me that place would be prison. Here I have learned to listen to the Lord.

None of us can go back. But we can all look forward to what lies ahead. We can choose God today and every day. Trusting God each day is living in freedom.

Prayer: *Dear God, thank you for the freedom that you have given us through the life, death and resurrection of your Son, Jesus Christ. Amen*

Thought for the day: God can set me free.

Nicholas Patterson (Florida, US)

Not alone in sorrow

Read Joshua 4:1–7

Jesus wept.
John 11:35 (KJV)

I went to church feeling numb, after hearing the news that eleven people had died in a shooting at a synagogue in nearby Pittsburgh, during a Shabbat service. I wanted to kneel at the altar and grieve over that hate-filled act while surrounded by people of faith. Someone handed me a small round stone as I entered the church.

Our minister invited us to lay our stones on the altar and demonstrate with a physical act our faith in God and his faithfulness to all generations. Our pastor's idea to place stones on the altar was inspired by the Jewish tradition of placing stones on graves. Stones remain long after flowers wilt, through the storms and chill of winter while we await the return of warm, sunny days. As I went up to the altar, I felt the warm stone in my hand. Then I released it and knelt with my friends, praying at the altar rail for our fractured world.

I left church that morning still in sorrow but assured once again that God understands our hurts and grieves with us. In the same way, God calls us to enter into the sorrow and suffering of all our neighbours, even those we have not met.

Prayer: *Everlasting God, thank you for your Holy Spirit, who walks with us through valleys of despair. Empower us to walk in love alongside others. Amen*

Thought for the day: God weeps with me in my suffering.

Jan Woodard (Pennsylvania, US)

PRAYER FOCUS: VICTIMS OF GUN VIOLENCE

Here I am

Read Mark 14:32–36

Many plans are in a person's mind, but the Lord's purpose will succeed.
Proverbs 19:21 (CEB)

My dream has always been to work for one of the world peace organisations, and I prayed that God would help me to do so. Because I knew that having experience would make it easier to find a job, I planned to volunteer with the organisation I hoped would hire me.

I was happy when I got a call from the organisation inviting me to apply for a position. I was called back for the second, third and final stages of the selection process. I felt confident that I would be accepted. But finally they chose one of the other candidates. I was disappointed and angry. This was the dream for which I had spent so much time and energy preparing.

Two months later, I learned of a Christian institution working for disadvantaged children. Though I was disappointed that God had not helped me achieve my original dream, I still feel that he wants me to serve others who are less fortunate than I am. I decided to apply, trusting that God knows what is best for my life. If I am not selected, it's okay. Here I am, God. Use me.

Prayer: *Dear Lord, give us courage to serve you in whatever ways and places we can, on every step of our journey. Amen*

Thought for the day: God's plans for me may be bigger and better than my plans for myself.

Yanti H. Damanik (West Java, Indonesia)

Friends who encourage

Read 1 Peter 5:6–11

The God of all grace, who called you to his eternal glory in Christ, after you have suffered a little while, will himself restore you and make you strong, firm and steadfast.
1 Peter 5:10 (NIV)

Sherry and I have been lifelong friends even when hundreds of miles separated us. When I was diagnosed with breast cancer for the second time and told that my uncertain future would be filled with months of chemotherapy and radiation, I was overwhelmed with anxiety and fear. My prayers seemed to go unheard.

Then I received a card from Sherry. Inside she had written, '1 Peter 5'. I quickly turned to my Bible. I scanned the passage searching for some solace or direction. When I read the verse quoted above, I felt Sherry's note was God's answer to my prayers. The scripture passage reminded me that God loved me and in time would once again use me for his glory.

A few months later Sherry suffered a debilitating stroke. Now it was my turn to offer support and encouragement. I sent her 1 Peter 5! In the following months, Sherry and I have thanked God for our long friendship and the encouragement we give each other by sharing comforting words and our favourite Bible verses. Just when we need God most, faithful friends can help reconnect us to him.

Prayer: *Dear God, thank you for your word that we can share and use to encourage each other. Help us to use our suffering for your glory. Amen*

Thought for the day: I can offer God's encouraging word to others during challenging times.

Carolyn Ellis (Tennessee, US)

First and last

Read Matthew 20:20–28
Whoever wishes to be great among you must be your servant, and whoever wishes to be first among you must be your slave; just as the Son of Man came not to be served but to serve.
Matthew 20:26–28 (NRSV)

Growing up, my brother and I had an ongoing dispute as to who was the favourite child. As the firstborn, I thought I had an edge. I'd been around the longest. But Steve, younger by four years and the only son and grandson, could rightly claim his own special place in our family.

My grandmother refused to succumb to our persistent efforts to choose which one of us was her favourite grandchild. My brother and I would find a time when Grandma wasn't surrounded by rival grandchildren and ask, 'Grandma, who is your favourite?' My grandmother's typical response, always offered with a smile, was, 'You are my bestest and my worsest.'

Many years later, the memory of this silly bit of dialogue still causes my brother and me to smile. It was the perfect non-answer to an unfair question. It reminds me of a story from Matthew's gospel. The mother of James and John wanted Jesus to favour her sons in the coming kingdom. Jesus pointed out that her request had significant consequences.

So much of life is like this: we have a sense that we should be a favoured child of God, perhaps at the expense of another. Grandma had a way of reminding us just how much we were loved, not only by her but by God, who created all of us.

Prayer: *Dear God, thank you for loving all your children. Teach us to do the same. Amen*

Thought for the day: In God's eyes, I am loved.

Ricki Aiello (Connecticut, US)

Gratitude

Read Psalm 30:4–12

Rejoice always, pray continually, give thanks in all circumstances; for this is God's will for you in Christ Jesus.

1 Thessalonians 5:16–18 (NIV)

I began the Camino de Santiago, the Way of Saint James, weighed down by issues in my life and with a deep sense of tiredness. My spouse and I had decided to undertake this journey to have some time out of our frantic everyday lives. We hoped to rest, be restored and listen to what God wanted to tell us, as thousands of people have done on this pilgrimage over the centuries. As we walked, I sensed God whispering 'gratitude' to me over and over again. It wasn't the message I was expecting or even looking for, but it was clear.

As the days passed, a deep sense of gratitude for my family, my friends, my life, my home, our country and even my struggles started to settle deep in my soul. I have come to realise how gratitude can lead us to fulfilment and ultimately to joy in our lives.

Prayer: *Dear God, open our eyes to all that we have to be grateful for. Thank you for awakening a sense of gratitude in our hearts. Amen*

Thought for the day: God has given me much to be grateful for.

Jess Gunning (Ballito, South Africa)

No hurry

In John 11, Jesus receives word that his friend Lazarus is ill. Instead of rushing to Lazarus' bedside to heal him, verse 6 says that Jesus 'stayed where he was two more days' (NIV). In the meantime, Lazarus dies. Had I been one of the disciples, I would have had difficulty understanding why Jesus didn't drop what he was doing and set out for Bethany immediately. There was, however, a point to Jesus' delay: 'that God's Son may be glorified through it' (v. 4) and 'that [the disciples] may believe' (v. 15). The time was of no consequence to Jesus, who went on to raise Lazarus and teach us something in the process – namely, it's not only the end result that matters but also what we learn in the time it takes to get there.

There's something to be said for proceeding steadily but not quickly. I drive an hour each morning to get to my office, and my commute covers long stretches of rural roads. I am not a slow driver, but I am also not a fast one. I take my time and I enjoy the drive – watching the sun rise over the hills, allowing my mind to go wherever it pleases. My early-morning commute is also a time for introspection, a time to consider my life. I value my drive for what it has taught me about the joy of not being in too big a hurry.

I do, however, tend to rush at other times. When I was at college, I couldn't wait for my time there to end. It was not an altogether pleasant experience; I thought the faster it went, the quicker I could move on to a phase of life that seemed more appealing – one without lectures, essays and late-night studying for exams. Looking back, I wish I had listened more carefully to the lectures, read some of the books more thoroughly and paid closer attention to the people around me. Had I seen then as clearly as I do now, that what happens on the journey is as important as reaching the destination, I might have spent less mental energy being frustrated by the pace. I might have freed my mind to be more attentive to and grateful for the self-discovery I was gaining in the process.

While the journey between life's milestones is important, so too are the much shorter distances we traverse each day – the time we stand waiting to order a cup of coffee, the duration of a dull meeting, the afternoon bus ride home. I want to take my time with the same confidence Jesus had getting to Lazarus. I don't get the sense that Jesus wasted that time, but instead he used it intentionally. The story reminds me that there is value in not being in a hurry – that no matter where we are on the journey, there is a lesson to be learned in the moment. When things are going slower than I would like, I ask myself, 'What am I not paying attention to that I should? What is this supposed to teach me? What is God trying to tell me?' Even – perhaps especially – in the delay, there's something to learn.

Several meditations in this issue address slowing down and learning a lesson from the moment at hand. You may want to read again the meditations for 4, 10, 14, 27 and 29 September; 7, 10, 14, 17, 26 and 28 October; 15 November; and 15, 19, 22 and 30 December, before responding to the reflection questions below.

QUESTIONS FOR REFLECTION

1 When have you rushed through a situation or experience only to later wish you had slowed down? What did you learn from that experience?

2 Read John 11:1–44. What stands out to you the most in this story? Do you think the outcome might have been different had Jesus gone to Bethany immediately? Explain.

3 In what circumstances is it easiest for you to be present and attentive? At what times is it most difficult?

Andrew Garland Breeden
Acquisitions Editor

Wonderfully made

Read Psalm 139:1–14

I praise you because I am fearfully and wonderfully made; your works are wonderful, I know that full well.

Psalm 139:14 (NIV)

Growing up as a dark-skinned boy, I endured constant pain from bullies who would call me 'charcoal boy'. These taunts seriously affected my self-esteem and self-confidence. I would come home from school dejected and in tears. I became angry with God for making me dark and – as I thought at the time – ugly. I was envious of my lighter-skinned friends. I struggled to accept myself.

Now, I know better: God is black. God is fair. God is short. God is tall. God is man. God is woman. I believe so because God made us and exclaimed that we are very good.

Foretelling the coming of Jesus, the Messiah, the Bible says, 'He grew up before him like a tender shoot, and like a root out of dry ground. He had no beauty or majesty to attract us to him, nothing in his appearance that we should desire him' (Isaiah 53:2).

When we reject our own or someone else's physical appearance, we reject God's wonderful creation. Regardless of how we look, we are beautiful and precious in God's sight, made in his image. Praise God, for we are fearfully and wonderfully made!

Prayer: *O Lord, thank you for making us in your wonderful image. When the world makes us doubt it, remind us of our beauty as your children. Amen*

Thought for the day: I am a beautiful creation of God.

Wati Longs (Nagaland, India)

A new way to serve

Read 2 Corinthians 5:18–20

'My only aim is to finish the race and complete the task the Lord Jesus
has given me – the task of testifying to the good news of God's grace.'
Acts 20:24 (NIV)

When I became a Christian 25 years ago, I took seriously Jesus' words
in Matthew 28:19: 'Go and make disciples of all nations.' I worked as an
interpreter with the many foreign missionaries who came to my home
town of Saint Petersburg, Russia.

When I moved to the United States, my interpretation ministry
ended. I was living on a farm and raising four children; I could not take
on any mission work. I read Galatians 6:2, 'Carry each other's burdens,'
and I asked God to reveal ways I could work for others and for him.

Soon I learned about a woman making quilts and selling them at
a charity auction. Proceeds from the auction would be used to build
wells in arid areas. I believed that God wanted me to help this woman
in her work by giving her several boxes of quilt fabric. Later I learned
that the quilt made out of my fabric was sold for the sum necessary to
build one well. I praised the Lord, who not only calls us to participate in
mission but also shows each of us unique ways to do so.

Prayer: *Dear Lord, help us to understand how we can help to share
your good news with all people. In Jesus' name. Amen*

Thought for the day: God can show me new ways to serve.

Tatiana Claudy (Indiana, US)

Drenched in grace

Read 2 Kings 5:1–14

Create in me a pure heart, O God, and renew a steadfast spirit within me.
Psalm 51:10 (NIV)

In today's reading, Naaman went to Elisha hoping to be healed of leprosy. Naaman was disappointed when Elisha conveyed a message through his servant to wash seven times in the river in order to be healed. The instructions sounded like a joke. But Naaman's servants reminded him that he would have been willing to follow complicated instructions, and questioned why he wouldn't perform the simple task requested of him. After following Elisha's orders, Naaman came out of the water of the Jordan healed and rejoicing.

As a widow who is well acquainted with the 'disease' of loneliness, I know how quickly it can sap my spirit. My mind can be overcome with longing for someone or something to make me feel less lonely. The story of Naaman reminds me that the remedy for loneliness is not found by seeking noteworthy objects or accomplishing grand tasks. My loneliness can be cured by simply drenching myself in God's river of grace.

I have found that the best way to 'drench' myself is to pray Psalm 51:10 regularly. This practice brings me out of my loneliness in a joyful state of mind – dripping with grace and restored in mind and spirit.

Prayer: *Healer of our souls, teach us to soak ourselves in your grace during our times of need. Renew a steadfast spirit within us. Amen*

Thought for the day: Praying the words of scripture leads me to God's grace.

Virginia Jelinek (Texas, US)

A spiritual plumb

Read 1 John 3:16–24

If we live by the Spirit, let us also be guided by the Spirit.
Galatians 5:25 (NRSV)

When I was a teenager, my father often took me to help him in his work of bricklaying. While helping him, the instruments that most fascinated me were the plumb and the level. A plumb is a type of pendulum, and a level is a kind of ruler with a reservoir filled with liquid. We would use the plumb to make sure the wall was aligned vertically and the level to make sure it was aligned horizontally.

Both instruments are crucial in determining the alignment of a house or wall. A structure must have good vertical and horizontal alignments in order to remain standing for a long time. If either alignment is ignored, a structure cannot withstand temperature changes, strong winds or water.

We can think about our relationships in similar terms. Our relationship with God shapes the kind of relationships we have with others. And we need a spiritual plumb and level to help us remain in right relationship with God and others. The word of God, prayer and remaining in communion with Christ act as our plumb and level and help keep us aligned.

Prayer: *Blessed God, help us to make our lives aligned and strong by our relationship with you.*

Thought for the day: I can deepen my relationship with God by staying in regular contact with him.

Domingos José Cazombo (Luanda, Angola)

Watered by the word

Read Psalm 1:1–6

They are like trees planted by streams of water, which yield their fruit in its season, and their leaves do not wither.
Psalm 1:3 (NRSV)

In the spring of 2017, tour groups from all over the world were drawn to a desert area in the United States. The attraction was the radiant carpets of wildflowers that had not been seen in 20 years. Seeds that had been dormant for decades for lack of water had germinated because of an unusually wet winter. This resulted in fields of brilliant orange poppies, desert lilies, blazing stars and the tall, spiny ocotillo.

How vital water is to our existence! In today's reading, the psalmist uses the analogy of water to teach us how to be spiritually healthy and productive. Those who study God's word and follow his law will thrive and bear fruit. Without the word, they would be like the desert in a dry year.

How well do I keep my soul watered? What seeds lie dormant in my heart for lack of spiritual water? If I watered those seeds by meditating on the word of God, what beauty might I bring to a dry and thirsty world?

Prayer: *Thank you, God, for the privilege of serving you. Help us to refresh a spiritually dry and thirsty world. Amen*

Thought for the day: What part of my spiritual life needs to be watered?

Madeline Peterson (Nebraska, US)

Taken away

Read Isaiah 6:1–7

The seraph touched my mouth with [a live coal] and said: 'Now that this has touched your lips, your guilt has departed and your sin is blotted out.'
Isaiah 6:7 (NRSV)

As I write this, I have 246 days remaining until I am released from prison. In preparation for my return to society, I pray that God will help me release my guilt. I know that I must do so in order to live an abundant life and find peace and joy.

I think of Isaiah, who felt guilty as he stood before God. Isaiah said, 'I am ruined! For I am a man of unclean lips' (Isaiah 6:5, NIV). But scripture says that Isaiah's sins were blotted out. Once God took away Isaiah's guilt, Isaiah was ready to go and do God's work.

Guilt can be all-consuming. It is like a chain that keeps us in one place, unable to move forward. With guilt, we may struggle to find peace or joy; we might find it difficult to have healthy relationships; we might not live abundant lives; and we probably aren't able to participate fully in God's work. However, God can take away our guilt and break the chains that hold us back. When we release our guilt to God, we can be like Isaiah and live abundant lives, sent by God to do his work.

Prayer: *Dear God, thank you for taking away our guilt. Help us to do your work with confidence. Amen*

Thought for the day: God can free me to move forward with joy.

Steve Wakefield (Georgia, US)

Serving with sincerity

Read 1 Peter 4:1–11

If anyone serves, they should do so with the strength God provides, so that in all things God may be praised through Jesus Christ.
1 Peter 4:11 (NIV)

One of the leaders in my Christian fellowship asked if I wanted to serve in our church's Sunday school. At first I was reluctant because I had no experience of working with children. I had grown up in a non-Christian family and had not attended Sunday school as a child. But my leader encouraged me and convinced me to try.

I tried to serve with all my heart. After a while, I found that teaching the children was not as difficult as I had thought. It is fun and has its own challenges.

Serving others does not require us to have certain skills or even prior experience. Serving only requires a willing heart and a willingness to learn. When our hearts want to serve with love and sincerity, God can use us and will help us. We do not need to worry about whether we are capable or have everything we need in our ministry. If we joyfully do God's work, he will provide whatever we need. When we try our best, we can let God take care of the rest.

Prayer: *Dear God, thank you for opportunities to serve you. Teach us to love and serve those to whom you guide us. Amen*

Thought for the day: All I need to serve God is a sincere and loving heart.

Meliana Santoso (East Java, Indonesia)

Acts of love

Read John 13:31–35
'By this everyone will know that you are my disciples, if you love one another.'
John 13:35 (NIV)

When I was training to be a hospital nurse, I spent a few weeks working on the paediatric ward. One of the patients I took care of was a young girl with a burned arm. Each day I cared for her wound, removing the old bandage, washing her burn with saline solution and putting a new bandage on her arm. Every time I took care of the girl, I asked God to help me be gentle and kind to her. I told her how brave she was and that her arm was getting better and would soon be as good as new.

I took care of her for only about a week. On my last day on that ward, I was saying goodbye to my patients. The girl motioned for me to bend down next to her. She kissed me on the cheek and said, 'Thank you.'

Although that was 40 years ago, I still remember that little girl. Love and kindness are precious gifts that everyone can share with others. Jesus told his disciples that their love was the mark that the world would see. I tended the little girl's burned arm, but God gave me the love and kindness to minister to her in a gentle and kind manner. Because God loved me first, I am able to share his love with others.

Prayer: *Dear Lord, because you loved us first, we are able to love others. Help us to find opportunities to share your love every day. Amen*

Thought for the day: God's love can work through me all the time.

Michael A. Campbell (Tennessee, US)

God carries all

Read Psalm 23:1–3

[The Lord] restores my soul.
Psalm 23:3 (NRSV)

One night I woke up around midnight feeling anxious, and everything just snowballed from there. I was worrying about areas of my life where I felt like a failure. My long list of responsibilities loomed over me, and I could not find peace. Finally, I prayed for God's help, and Psalm 23 came to mind. This psalm has always been a soothing balm for me as I visualise God's green pastures and still waters. But this time God showed me something different.

Verses 2 and 3 do not begin with the pronoun 'I' but with the pronoun 'he', meaning God. While I had been wrestling with all the things that I had not been doing, the psalm was showing me that God is the one who is in charge of the doing. I do not restore my own soul. I do not lead myself in paths of righteousness. I do not fulfil any of the promises here – not one! It is God who does the guiding, providing, restoring and all other good things. I had been struggling needlessly with burdens that were not mine to carry.

The heavy weights of worry and anxiety began to be replaced by peace, and I was able to go back to sleep. Nothing was left for me to worry over. God had it all covered.

Prayer: *Good shepherd, thank you for reminding us that we are not in charge. Help us to find peace in you. Amen*

Thought for the day: The shepherd carries all my burdens.

Belle Todd (Texas, US)

God's promises

Read 2 Peter 3:8–18

The Lord is not slow in keeping his promise, as some understand slowness. Instead he is patient with you, not wanting anyone to perish, but everyone to come to repentance.
2 Peter 3:9 (NIV)

As a teenager I was introduced to Alcoholics Anonymous (AA) through Al-Anon, a local fellowship that offers a programme of recovery for family and friends of alcoholics. My mum was an active contributor to the local Al-Anon support group and she brought me to meetings because of the deteriorating relationship between me and my dad, who was an alcoholic.

Throughout my adult life, I have overcome many trials and tribulations, including excessive drinking. I have attempted to make deals and to negotiate with God in exchange for a healthier and more abundant life. By the grace of God, I finally decided to address my excessive drinking by joining an AA programme.

This faith-based programme and my own spiritual journey have reaffirmed for me that God makes promises and keeps them. I now see my exposure to Al-Anon as a teenager as inspired by God, as it helped me know how to address my alcoholism. I trust God's words in Jeremiah 29:11, that he wants to give me hope and a future, because he revealed to me a path to salvation. We can trust God's promise to us: 'I will not leave you until I have done what I have promised you' (Genesis 28:15).

Prayer: *Dear God, you have always kept your promises. Help us to keep our promises to you, to ourselves and to others. Amen*

Thought for the day: I can trust in God's promises.

Kevin Gamble (Ohio, US)

Sharing the Spirit

Read 2 Kings 2:1–12

Elijah said to Elisha, 'Tell me what I may do for you, before I am taken from you.' Elisha said, 'Please let me inherit a double share of your spirit.'
2 Kings 2:9 (NRSV)

Recently, I received an email regarding a friend who was struggling with serious issues after surgery. 'Please join us in prayer tomorrow at 9.10 am,' the message said. Usually I would rather pray with someone face to face than online, but that day was different. Friends from all over responded to the call. They emailed, they tweeted and they posted the invitation on Facebook. Like all the others, I set a reminder to be in prayer at 9.10.

I thought of Elisha, who followed Elijah from Bethel to Jericho to the Jordan. Time and time again, people said to him, 'Do you know that today the Lord will take your master away from you?' And Elisha answered, 'Yes, I know; be silent.' True friends, no matter how far away they live, never leave us. They are there in joy and sorrow, in life and death.

When the time arrived, we gathered online to pray for our friend. Like Elisha, who begged for a double share of Elijah's spirit, we prayed that God would bless our friend with Christ's Spirit of eternal life. May we have the strength and courage always to be present, heart and soul, with those we love.

Prayer: *Dear God, grant us the guidance of your Spirit to remain faithful to family and friends. Amen*

Thought for the day: Prayer extends beyond all boundaries.

Patricia Marks (Georgia, US)

PRAYER FOCUS: ONLINE PRAYER COMMUNITIES

God's abiding love

Read Isaiah 41:8–10

*'Do not fear, for I am with you; do not be dismayed, for I am your God.
I will strengthen you and help you; I will uphold you with my righteous
right hand.'*
Isaiah 41:10 (NIV)

I was born with a withered Achilles tendon, and I walk with a limp.
My parents took me to many doctors in search of a remedy but to no
avail. Despairing, I concluded that I would walk with a limp for the rest
of my life.

When I was 15, I began suffering back pains. I told my mother I was
ready to see a specialist and that if I needed to undergo surgery, I would
be willing to endure it. She confided that my health had been the focus
of her constant prayers all these years.

Learning of my mother's constant prayers for me prompted me to
think about the ways God's provision has been evident throughout
my life – from the medical care I received to the resources needed for
the surgery, to allowing me to pursue my studies and be at the top of
my class. Today I am 22 years old. I praise and thank God because in
my disability I have gained a greater understanding of God's grace.
I will always depend on him and know that his power is made perfect
in weakness.

Prayer: *Creator God, thank you for guiding us in our daily journey and
for continuing to sustain us. Refresh our spirits with your abiding love.
Amen*

Thought for the day: God provides strength in weakness.

Isaías Natanael Parra Almeida (Pichincha, Ecuador)

Strong roots

Read Ezekiel 2:8—3:3
Happy are those who… delight… in the law of the Lord, and on his law they meditate day and night.
Psalm 1:1–2 (NRSV)

The young oak tree in our front garden was struggling. Battered by a hurricane, it was leaning to one side and on the verge of being uprooted. My husband and I had staked it to help it stand upright, but every time there was a strong wind we had to stake it again. Finally, after about three months, the root system became fully stable and the tree could stand alone.

Watching that tree endure the aftermath of the storm reminded me of the importance of staying grounded in the word of God on a daily basis. In Psalm 1, the writer calls us to meditate on God's word in order to bear good fruit that ripens and matures. The prophet Ezekiel spoke of eating the word so that it could feed and transform the Israelites into the people God created them to be.

Spiritual disciplines are the means of grace that enable us to send out deep roots that anchor us in God's word. The faithful practice of worship, prayer and service can help fuel the grace we need to thrive as workers with God. Then, as Jesus said in the sermon on the mount, we can shine brightly and our good works will glorify our Father in heaven (see Matthew 5:16).

Prayer: *Gracious Father, show us how to take in your word openly, humbly and attentively. In the name of Jesus. Amen*

Thought for the day: The Bible keeps me rooted in God, in whose image I was created.

Judith Brown (North Carolina, US)

Feed the hungry

Read Matthew 14:13–21

'Bring them here to me,' [Jesus] said… [The people] all ate and were satisfied.
Matthew 14:18, 20 (NIV)

My wife grew up in north-west Indiana. Her mother, Miriam, was a teacher and housewife, and her father, Henry, was a farmer and the local postmaster. Their modest home faced the railway tracks. In 1929, the United States stock market crashed, which contributed to an economic depression. Many people were out of work, and the economy did not begin to recover until years later. Many people had nowhere to live or sleep and some 'rode the rails', living in freight train carriages and stopping to eat where they could. Miriam always provided food and drink to those who turned up at her door. Soon word spread among the people on the trains that they could stop and be fed at her house.

Miriam lived out the message, 'Bring the hungry here to me, and I will feed them.' Miriam's story reminds me of the story of Jesus feeding the five thousand. Jesus fed the people who came to hear his message by turning five loaves of bread and two fish into enough food for everyone. While Miriam couldn't multiply her food, she knew that she could help to feed the hungry. And she did so in the name of Jesus.

Prayer: *Thank you, Lord, for people who care for others in your name. Help us to act when we see opportunities to serve others. Amen*

Thought for the day: What is God calling me to do to help feed those who are hungry?

Charles Heath (Hawaii, US)

Glimpses of God's power

Read Genesis 2:4–9, 15

What are human beings that you are mindful of them, mortals that you care for them? Yet you have made them a little lower than God, and crowned them with glory and honour.
Psalm 8:4–5 (NRSV)

Warm spring days often bring badgers out early, so my husband and I set out on our first badger watch of the year with great anticipation, hoping to catch sight of one. On this occasion, however, the badgers didn't come – but it wasn't a wasted evening. As I stood in silence, just waiting, I was struck by the brilliance of our creator.

I stood behind an enormous oak that hid me from view. I have read that oak trees can live up to a thousand years, and I felt dwarfed by its powers of endurance. Then I realised that as God looked at the scene, he placed significance on me, not the tree. God is the Ancient of Days, and that tree represents no more than a breath in God's eternal plan. Meanwhile, God's people are greatly valued, crowned with glory and honour. Like the psalmist, I wondered, 'Why us?'

I am astonished that God cares for us. As I spend time in the natural world, I am constantly rejoicing at how big God is and how incredible it is that he should delight in us.

Prayer: *Creator of all, we see your fingerprints throughout creation. Thank you for the daily encouragement this awareness gives us. Amen*

Thought for the day: In creation, I see just a small fragment of God's greatness.

Caroline Greville (England, United Kingdom)

What can I do?

Read Exodus 35:20–35

We, who are many, are one body in Christ, and individually we are members one of another. We have gifts that differ according to the grace given to us.
Romans 12:5–6 (NRSV)

I don't enjoy cooking or washing up. So when members of the church planned to prepare dinner for people before a special service, I didn't volunteer. But one day one of the organisers asked me, 'Are you going to be here to help?'

I told her I had somewhere else to be and could only attend the service after the meal. But as it turned out I arrived at church earlier than I expected, well before the service started. I went to the kitchen to see if I could help and found six stressed women struggling to finish everything in time to attend the service. 'What can I do?' I asked.

'The tables need cleaning,' one answered. 'I can do that,' I said, as I grabbed a cloth and began to clean the messy tables. To my surprise we finished on time, and I was glad I had offered to help.

That night reminded me of the Israelites building the tabernacle. Many willingly brought offerings. God gave specific talents to some, like Bezalel and Oholiab, engravers and embroiderers. Cleaning tables may not be as high on the gifted list as cooking for 200 hungry people, but it was part of the ministry. Each of us working together provided a good meal for people, who were then ready to feast their souls on God's word.

Prayer: *Gracious God, thank you for giving us abilities that we can use in your service. In Jesus' name. Amen*

Thought for the day: Each act of service I perform is a gift to God.

Lucinda J. Rollings (Indiana, US)

Humility

Read Philippians 2:3–11
Haughty eyes and a proud heart – the unploughed field of the wicked – produce sin.
Proverbs 21:4 (NIV)

One of my joys in retirement has been finding more time to read the Bible. I have been amazed by how many verses and stories pertain to humility. They have prompted me to reflect on how often my ego comes into play and manifests itself in negative ways. Pride has plagued humanity since the beginning. And our culture constantly bombards us with messages that speak about gratifying our desires through possessions, appearance or status.

What a contrast it is to reflect on the life of our Lord and Saviour! Though his coming was heralded for centuries, Jesus' arrival was humble: in a stable and surrounded by animals. Everything Jesus did during his time on earth reflected humility, including his choice of disciples and the people with whom he associated. His humility continued to the very end of his life on earth, when he submitted to the will of God, was arrested and tried as a criminal, then suffered torture and death on a cross.

Jesus' humble life provides a model for us to follow. Christ the King came not to be served, but to serve (see Matthew 20:28). We can embrace that attitude and strive to do the same.

Prayer: *Dear Lord, when our pride and ego rise up, help us instead to model our lives after the humble example of Christ. Amen*

Thought for the day: I will look for opportunities to follow the example of Jesus.

John D. Bown (Minnesota, US)

The card

Read Hebrews 10:19–25

Let us consider how we may spur one another on towards love and good deeds.
Hebrews 10:24 (NIV)

I am involved in two ministry activities at my church. It's not a large church, and it sometimes seems as though a relatively small number of people do most of the work. So it is easy to feel underappreciated and unsupported. I was feeling like this recently and was growing increasingly bitter at the idea that so few seem to care about the church's ministries. Then I received a thank-you card expressing gratitude for all my efforts and for my willingness to serve God. That card changed my attitude.

First, it took my eyes off myself and put them where they belong – on God and his sufficiency. Second, it lifted my lagging spirits. I faced my next church duties with a vigour I hadn't felt in a while. And third, it reminded me how vital it is to obey Hebrews 10:24: 'Let us consider how we may spur one another on towards love and good deeds.'

Spurring one another on can be as easy as an encouraging word after church, an email, a card or a phone call. It can even be anonymous! A simple 'I'm praying for you and the valuable service you are doing for the kingdom of God' can have a huge, positive impact on someone's life and faith. I know.

Prayer: *Dear Lord, keep us in tune with the needs of our brothers and sisters, and remind us to be generous with our encouragement. Amen*

Thought for the day: A kind word can make a huge difference in God's kingdom.

Esther MacDonald (Quebec, Canada)

Something new

Read 1 Peter 4:12–19

Dear friends, do not be surprised at the fiery ordeal that has come on you to test you, as though something strange were happening to you.
1 Peter 4:12 (NIV)

There is a legend about a cook preparing a meal one night about 2,000 years ago. As he stirred together a few ordinary kitchen ingredients, the mixture suddenly exploded, which led to the invention of fireworks.

Similarly, the unexpected hardships in my life have often led to the invention of something new in me. Though I may never fully understand why financial troubles or health issues arise, my hardships have humbled me and strengthened my character. They have opened my heart to see God's loving actions in my life, which time and time again have brought comfort and hope. I have learned to surrender more of myself to God when I face seemingly impossible circumstances. In turn, God has provided the guidance I desperately needed.

God knows how to blend the messy circumstances of our lives to help us grow. When we trust the Master Inventor to create something new from the explosions that disrupt our lives, personal growth can take place.

Prayer: *Dear God, thank you for your kindness and guidance through the unforeseen circumstances of our lives. Amen*

Thought for the day: Today I will look for evidence that God is creating something new in me.

Doug Lim (California, US)

A pillar of fire

Read Exodus 13:17–22

The Lord went ahead of them… by night in a pillar of fire to give them light.

Exodus 13:21 (NIV)

Garden bonfires are one of my favourite childhood memories. One evening recently, my neighbour had one in her garden. The air smelled like smoke from burning wood, and the dark summer sky glowed orange as flames crackled and popped. With the brilliant blaze emanating from my neighbour's garden, I reminisced about family gatherings and marshmallows toasted over a smouldering fire. I remember my father stoking the flames as a pillar of fire illuminated the sky.

Beyond my childhood memories, the bonfire brought to mind God guiding the Israelites at night in the desert. God became a 'pillar of fire to give them light' that kept 'its place in front of the people' (Exodus 13:21–22). The Israelites received God's guidance by following a pillar of fire.

We receive God's guidance by practising spiritual disciplines. When my husband had a heart attack, I was lost in a desert of fear and anxiety. I received God's guidance through prayer, memorising scripture and writing in my journal. These practices led me to God's calming peace so I could cope with my husband's illness. God's word promises that 'the Lord will guide you always' (Isaiah 58:11). Whatever challenge we're facing, when we ask God to send light and truth to guide us (see Psalm 43:3), his guiding light will shine on us.

Prayer: *Faithful God, thank you for your guidance as we traverse life's unfamiliar paths. Amen*

Thought for the day: What spiritual disciplines help me to follow God's light?

Debra Pierce (Massachusetts, US)

Forgiveness

Read Psalm 103:1–13

[The Lord] does not deal with us according to our sins, nor repay us according to our iniquities… As far as the east is from the west, so far he removes our transgressions from us.
Psalm 103:10, 12 (NRSV)

I've said and done many things I'm not proud of in my life. When I consider them, I wish I could go back in time and stop myself from committing them in the first place. But I cannot retract my hurtful words or actions, and I cannot reasonably anticipate forgiveness from those I have offended. However, I can make a commitment to do better going forward.

When I read Psalm 103, I imagine David isolated, living with the consequences of his own quite serious transgressions, for which he offers no excuses. The words of the psalm make me believe that David regretted his misbehaviour but took solace in knowing that God removes and casts our sins away from us 'as far as the east is from the west'. I like this perspective: that from God's viewpoint our sins are out of sight.

So when we have misgivings over our past sins, we don't have to dwell on them. Instead of living in fear of retribution, we can focus on God's loving mercy and kindness.

Prayer: *Loving God, thank you for your infinite patience and forgiveness. Help us to extend the same forgiveness to others that you have extended to us. Amen*

Thought for the day: No matter what happened in my past, God's loving mercy is for me.

Tom Johnson (Nevada, US)

New growth

Read Colossians 3:1–11

If anyone is in Christ, the new creation has come: the old has gone, the new is here!

2 Corinthians 5:17 (NIV)

One morning I looked at my flowerpots, and I was sad to see that they were neglected and overgrown with grass and weeds. I decided to tend to them, hoping to make them look more beautiful and well maintained. The growth of my plants had been stunted by the grass and weeds, so I pulled out all the weeds and added fertiliser to allow the plants to produce new, healthy growth.

When I had finished tidying up my flowerpots, I thought, 'It is the same with me spiritually. My life would be more beautiful if I were to get rid of the grass and weeds in me.' Worry, disappointment and heartache can consume me. These 'grasses' and 'weeds' make it difficult for me to grow into a new creation in God. It is not always easy, but I want to continue to grow in faith so that I can glorify God through my life. I hope that as God's children we can all welcome new growth in our faith and our lives.

Prayer: *Heavenly Father, thank you for encouraging us to grow. Help us as we strive to do our best for you. In the name of Jesus, who taught us to pray, 'Father, hallowed be your name, your kingdom come. Give us each day our daily bread. Forgive us our sins, for we also forgive everyone who sins against us. And lead us not into temptation.'* Amen*

Thought for the day: What do I need to clear away so that I can grow spiritually today?

Merry Gultom (West Java, Indonesia)

God's favour

Read James 4:13–17

You do not even know what will happen tomorrow. What is your life?
James 4:14 (NIV)

During my training as a teacher, I had to implement a reward programme in a class I taught. Pupils earned extra points for good behaviour and excellent work. These were traded in on selected days for small prizes and privileges. My students quickly became obsessed with the rewards.

But I struggled as I watched the frustrated faces of students who failed to meet the academic and behavioural standards. The day after I finished collecting data to complete my class requirements, I ended the reward programme. A student who struggled with reading came to me and said, 'Thanks. I hated that points system.' Much of society says that we gain power, possessions and privileges by how we look, act and perform – but that is not how we gain God's favour.

Not long ago, four words from James 4:14 caught my attention: 'What is your life?' When I thought about my life, I realised it was time to re-evaluate some of my choices. I prayed for guidance to know what to do with my God-given resources and how to follow his will in using them. I often recall those four words. They are a reminder that my life must embrace knowing and following God's will.

Prayer: *Dear God, grant us the strength to resist the appeals of worldly influences and learn to live for your purposes. Help us to understand your will for our lives. Amen*

Thought for the day: I do not have to earn God's favour.

Nancy Lewis Shelton (Missouri, US)

All God's children

Read Matthew 22:34–40

There is no longer Jew or Greek, there is no longer slave or free, there is no longer male and female; for all of you are one in Christ Jesus.
Galatians 3:28 (NRSV)

In the mid-1950s, I was a teenager working with some men loading trucks with foodstuffs. We were working hard lifting heavy crates. Eventually we stopped for lunch. We all sat down at one big table, but the man who owned the restaurant came to us and said, 'I can't serve that black man who is with you; he will have to eat at the back.' I asked, 'Why? Lafayette has been working with us all morning.' The owner replied, 'He can't eat in here.' We asked the restaurant owner if we could all eat at the back together. When he said yes, we all moved to the back room.

That encounter upset me and has stayed with me all my life. Paul wrote in Galatians 3:28 that we are all one in Christ. We are black, white and a lot of other shades in between; and God created all of us. Knowing this and remembering Jesus' commandment in Matthew 22:37–39, shouldn't we all go out of our way to treat each other with love and respect? After all, we are all children of God.

Prayer: *Dear God, help us to recognise discrimination and to go out of our way to treat one another with love and respect. Amen*

Thought for the day: Whenever I see discrimination against one of God's children, I will speak up.

Jon C. Goeringer (Maryland, US)

Every step

Read Philippians 3:12–14
The steadfast love of the Lord never ceases, his mercies never come to an end; they are new every morning.
Lamentations 3:22–23 (NRSV)

I wear a fitness tracker on my wrist that logs the steps I take each day. Some days – like the time my family and I walked more than 30,000 steps in New York City – I exceed my daily goal of 10,000 steps. But most days I fall way short. I often glance at my total step count at the end of the day and wish I had tried harder to meet my goal. But every morning the step counter begins at zero. No matter what my count was the day before – 2,000 or 200,000 – the next day is always a clean slate.

My walk with God is a lot like that. Some days I walk closely with God, aligning my steps with his. Those are great days! But sometimes I follow my own agenda, barely checking to see if I am following God's path. The good news is that every day begins with a clean slate. If I've had a great day with God, I can't rest and coast through the next day – the count is at zero, and I have work to do for the kingdom. Similarly, on the days when I struggle in my walk with God, I can go to sleep knowing that tomorrow is a brand-new day.

Prayer: *Dear God, thank you for walking with us every day. Help us to align our steps with yours. Amen*

Thought for the day: Each day is a new chance to walk with God.

Carolyn Chapman (Missouri, US)

Always grateful

Read Luke 17:11–19

One of them, when he saw he was healed, came back, praising God in a loud voice. He threw himself at Jesus' feet and thanked him.
Luke 17:15–16 (NIV)

In several countries around the world, including my home country of Brazil, people celebrate a day of thanksgiving. In the United States, Thanksgiving Day brings together family members, friends and neighbours.

However, we don't always find it easy or remember to express our gratitude. In today's reading, Jesus had healed ten lepers, but only one of them thanked him. Jesus asked, 'Where are the other nine?'

We are invited to be grateful to God, not just on a special day or at mealtime, but always. We are called to live life as an expression of gratitude for what God has done and will do, and for Christ who is with us in all circumstances. When we have grateful hearts, we can welcome God's love and feel his welcome for us. Then as a response to God's love, we can make our lives, work and service all offerings of thanks to him.

Prayer: *We are grateful, O God, for all that you are and all that you do. Give us a constant spirit of gratitude to you and one another, offering our lives and talents to you and our neighbours. Amen*

Thought for the day: With a grateful heart, I can serve God and my neighbours.

Nelson Luiz Campos Leite (São Paulo, Brazil)

Power in weakness

Read 2 Corinthians 12:6–10

[The Lord] said to [Paul], 'My grace is sufficient for you, for my power is made perfect in weakness.'
2 Corinthians 12:9 (NIV)

There's an old spiritual that begins: 'I don't feel no ways tired.' The song goes on to say that even though the road is not easy, God has been with us until now and will not abandon us.

I wish I could say that the words of this song ring true for me all the time, but the truth is that sometimes I do get tired along my Christian journey. In fact, I admit that at times I have felt that God did leave me. But thankfully reality always sets in, and I realise that it's me – operating in my own strength, with my own agenda and my flawed human-ness – who has left God.

In truth, it is when I am tired and feeling alone that I should be most dependent on God. Paul confirms this in our reading for today: '[The Lord] said to me, "My grace is sufficient for you, for my power is made perfect in weakness."'

In those moments when I'm feeling defeated, I can find peace in the presence of God. My weariness never lasts because God, at the right time, steps in to surround me with love – love that will never let me go. Then I know that God didn't bring me this far to leave me.

Prayer: *O Lord, when we grow weary, give us strength to continue, knowing your love and power will sustain us. Amen*

Thought for the day: God can turn my weariness into worship.

Kathy Gaillard (Wisconsin, US)

God helps

Read Psalm 121:1–8

My help comes from the Lord, the maker of heaven and earth.
Psalm 121:2 (CEB)

When I worked for the Gujarat Tract and Book Society, I was responsible for the distribution, promotion and sales of literature. I once visited a church in South Gujarat to preach and to promote publications, including the Gujarati edition of *The Upper Room*. Early in the morning, when I reached the village, I needed to get to the church but had heavy parcels of literature with me. Waiting for a vehicle to take me to the church, I began to worry that I would be late. So I started praying for help.

As I prayed, I saw a young man passing by on a motorbike. He stopped near me and asked if I wanted a lift to the church. I said yes, and he helped me reach my destination on time. The minister welcomed me, and after the church service many people bought literature and Bibles, and many subscribed to *The Upper Room*.

I thanked God for helping me that day by sending that young man to get me to the church. As the psalmist reminds us, '[Our] help comes from the Lord.'

Prayer: *Heavenly Father, thank you for the people you send to help us. Thank you for all the blessings you give us every day. Amen*

Thought for the day: Help from God comes in a variety of ways.

Chhotubhai Parmar (Gujarat, India)

Broken people

Read Matthew 1:18–23

God so loved the world that he gave his one and only Son, that whoever believes in him shall not perish but have eternal life.
John 3:16 (NIV)

At the beginning of Advent, I brought my nativity set out of the attic to put on display and was sad to find that many of the figures were broken. The angel had only half a wing, the shepherd was missing a hand, a wise man had no foot and the donkey had one lone ear. Only baby Jesus was intact and appeared unharmed. I'm not sure what happened. The figures were fine when I packed them away last January.

Initially I thought of purchasing a new nativity set. Then I realised that maybe God had a message for me. We are all broken people. But God can accomplish great works through us. When we repent of our sins and ask for forgiveness, God can give us new life despite our brokenness. Jesus' birth was all about bringing new life to the world.

I think that I will continue to display my imperfect nativity set as a reminder of God's great love for me. God loves us so much that Jesus came to take on the brokenness of this world by being born as a tiny baby. Through Jesus' willingness to live a human life, we have the hope of eternal life. Isn't this what Christmas is all about?

Prayer: *Dear God, thank you for loving us so much that you sent Jesus into the world so that we can have eternal life. Amen*

Thought for the day: Though I am broken, God loves me and can use me to accomplish great things.

Susan L. Stombaugh (Ohio, US)

A generous gift

Read John 21:15–17

Let each of you look not to your own interests, but to the interests of others. Let the same mind be in you that was in Christ Jesus.
Philippians 2:4–5 (NRSV)

I volunteer with an organisation that provides meals to people in need. One day when I delivered a meal to Tom, I noticed a repairman approaching the home next door.

I learned that Tom had secretly paid to have his neighbours' broken hot water heater replaced, knowing that the family was unemployed, had young children and had no funds to cover such a cost. I asked Tom why he didn't tell the family about his generous act, and he replied, 'Because I want the credit to go to the Lord, not me.'

Tom has a variety of health issues and lives with few amenities. He has a strong and abiding faith in Jesus Christ. For me, Tom's kind act and humility are perfect examples of what it means to be a Christian. If we wish to claim that title, we must consider how we will tend to Christ's lambs and feed God's sheep. By following in Christ's footsteps, we can extend God's blessings to others and show by example, with kind words and actions, the love of God for all people.

Prayer: *Gracious Lord, help us to glorify you as we serve others. Amen*

Thought for the day: When done in love, my acts of service reflect God's mercy and grace.

Robert E. Boertien (Oregon, US)

The blue hyacinth

Read 1 Thessalonians 5:12–21

Rejoice always, pray continually, give thanks in all circumstances; for this is God's will for you in Christ Jesus.
1 Thessalonians 5:16–18 (NIV)

As I was walking through my neighbourhood, I noticed a neglected garden, full of weeds and dry soil. Then in a corner I spotted a beautiful blue hyacinth. It reminded me of the saying, 'Bloom where you are planted.' At times in my life that saying has encouraged me – times when I have found myself in a place or situation where I have not chosen to be. In such a time and place it's easy for me to give in to self-pity and complaining. The better choice, however, is to bloom and flourish.

For me, the verses from 1 Thessalonians quoted above provide a model for how we can thrive in difficult situations – whether they are related to work, finances, relationships, health or home. First, we can think about all we have in Jesus to be joyful about. Second, we can pray constantly, honestly telling God our feelings and asking for his help. After all, nothing lasting can be achieved on our own. Third, Paul says we are to be thankful for all the gifts God gives us each day. Joy returns when we praise God, who loves us wherever we are, no matter where we are planted.

Prayer: *Loving God, thank you for your constant goodness. Be with us wherever we are today, and grant us joy and a thankful heart so that our lives honour you. Amen*

Thought for the day: I can find joy in any circumstance by giving praise to God.

Ann Stewart (South Australia, Australia)

A firm place

Read Matthew 7:21–29

'The rain fell, the floods came, and the winds blew and beat on that house, but it did not fall, because it had been founded on rock.'
Matthew 7:25 (NRSV)

Years ago my wife and I received an ornamental wrought-iron and wooden bench as a gift. We placed it outside in a spot that was good for people-watching or personal reflection. But over the years, we forgot about the bench until it was time to move. We moved it three times to new homes where it would sit out in the elements, and slowly it fell into disrepair. The wooden parts began to rot, and some of the nuts and bolts fell out; but the wrought iron was still strong. One day my wife and I decided to refurbish the bench. When we had finished, it looked almost new and made our entire garden look better!

Now I think about how that bench reflects my journey of faith. As a child I started out with a sturdy love of God. As I grew up, I went down another path, assuming that what the world thought was acceptable had to be right. My sturdy love of God fell into disrepair. Fortunately I still had my wrought-iron frame of growing up in a home where God, church and family were important. This has allowed me to begin the repair of my faith – to become more obedient to God, my family and my church. My faith is now a firm place where I can rest and know the love of God.

Prayer: *Heavenly Father, thank you for the sturdy framework of faith and Christian community that shapes our lives. Amen*

Thought for the day: God's love is the sturdy frame that can hold together faith that is in disrepair.

Chris Mewhirter (Nebraska, US)

The heart of the matter

Read Acts 1:15–17, 20–26

'Lord, you know everyone's heart.'
Acts 1:24 (NIV)

As a teenager, I struggled with acne. Every morning I obsessed over how to cover new spots on my face. I avoided getting too close when speaking with strangers, thinking they might be repulsed by my face. I prayed every night for God to take away my defects because I wanted people to like me. I saw myself through the eyes of others.

Over the years, my faith grew and my prayers changed, even though I continued to struggle with acne. I stopped pleading with God to give me a glowing complexion because I trusted that he loved me just the way he had created me. All creation meets God's standards of perfection and beauty, and that includes me.

After Jesus' ascension into heaven, when the disciples wanted to choose someone to replace Judas Iscariot, they asked God, 'Lord, you know everyone's heart. Show us which one of these two you have chosen' (Acts 1:24). Matthias was chosen, just as David was chosen: each for his heart.

God knows my thoughts, desires, plans and ambitions. He is concerned with the condition of my heart – not my skin, weight, hair or nails. Instead of fretting about how I look, I begin each day by meditating on God's word and praying for more love, more faith and more of God in my heart.

Prayer: *Dear God, help us to value in ourselves what matters most to you. Help us to love and serve you without reservation. Amen*

Thought for the day: I will value in myself what God values – my heart.

Mabel Ninan (California, US)

Prompting

Read John 14:15–27

'The Holy Spirit, whom the Father will send in my name, will teach you all things and will remind you of everything I have said to you.'
John 14:26 (NIV)

Years ago, my family and I decided to foster young girls. Each time a girl returned to her parents or guardians, we felt the Holy Spirit leading us through the bittersweet moment. But after a while, we were emotionally spent, and I decided not to accept any more foster children.

Then one day a social worker called me at the school where I teach to ask if I could foster a four-year-old girl whose siblings had been placed with other foster families. I told the social worker I could not and hung up.

When I returned to my classroom, feeling distressed, one of my students gave me a big hug and said, 'Teacher, you are so good.' I felt like someone had thrown a bucket of cold water in my face. Me, good? I had just said no to helping a four-year-old child. It felt like the prompting of the Holy Spirit, so I called the social worker and said I would accept the child if they would work quickly to find her a permanent home.

A permanent placement with a different family never happened. It has been 14 years since the prompting of the Holy Spirit brought that small, fragile child into our home. She has grown into a beautiful young woman who has brought our family many blessings and has enriched our lives.

Prayer: *Gracious God, help us to discern the prompting of the Holy Spirit and to care for the most vulnerable among us. In Jesus' name, we pray. Amen*

Thought for the day: I serve Christ when I heed the prompting of the Holy Spirit.

Ana Sylvia Pedroza R. (Puerto Rico, US)

Press pause

Read Mark 6:7–13, 30–31
[Jesus] went up on a mountainside to pray.
Mark 6:46 (NIV)

In our fast-paced, busy and loud world, we may find it challenging to rest. Overwhelming needs – spiritual, physical, emotional and mental – surround us. We can easily fall into a pattern of constant 'doing' because of the great need in the world.

Yet Jesus took time away from his work to focus on his relationship with God. And he taught this truth to the disciples. In Mark 6 we read how Jesus sent the disciples on a mission trip. Upon their return, he could have sent them to a new place to preach and perform miracles. Instead, he told them they needed time away to rest.

I have noticed that the more I do at the expense of my time in communion with God, the more likely I am to be stressed or overwhelmed. However, when I take time to pause and rest in my relationship with God, my renewed spirit helps me do his work in a way that cannot happen when I'm always on the move. I'm continuing to learn from the Master Teacher that I cannot run on empty – physically or spiritually.

Prayer: *Dear Father, help us to follow the example of Jesus, who taught us that to be effective disciples we need rest. Help us as we seek to make resting with you a regular practice in our lives. Amen*

Thought for the day: My service is stronger when I make time to rest with God.

Kyle Bjerga (Illinois, US)

Not alone

Read Isaiah 35:1–10

The body does not consist of one member but of many.
1 Corinthians 12:14 (NRSV)

I look forward to worshipping with my local congregation. I particularly love the special seasons of the church year, and I most want to be in church during Advent. The songs, the Bible readings, the sermons and the music herald the coming of our Lord.

Last Advent, health problems kept me from attending services for several weeks. I felt alone and discouraged even though I knew my church family was praying for me. Sitting at home on a Sunday morning and feeling removed from worship, I did what always encourages me – I opened my Bible.

As I read God's word, I felt encouraged. I wasn't alone after all! I realised again that I am part of a larger community, the body of Christ, and that a body of believers all over the world was joining together to celebrate the Lord's coming. I lit my Advent candles, played my favourite hymns and celebrated the Lord's birth with my family in Christ all over the world.

Prayer: *Dear God, thank you for the community we find in you. Help us to feel connected to all our brothers and sisters in Christ, especially when we feel alone. Amen*

Thought for the day: No matter where I am, I am part of the body of Christ.

DeVonna R. Allison (Florida, US)

Solid ground

Read Luke 6:46–49

'They are like a man building a house, who dug down deep and laid the foundation on rock. When the flood came, the torrent struck that house but could not shake it.'

Luke 6:48 (NIV)

In the process of building our new church hall, we encountered problems with the foundation for the building. Without a solid foundation, the building would eventually develop weaknesses and the structure would not be supported. But the issue was resolved, and we now have a beautiful building for our church and community.

This reminded me of the solid foundation we need in our relationship with God. Without this foundation, our faith, trust and hope would eventually erode – we would become ineffective in our Christian life and in our relationship with God.

We can reinforce our spiritual foundation through daily devotions, reading scripture, worshipping with fellow believers and building a personal relationship with God. Scripture tells us that those who build their house on sand will not hold up under the floods that are sure to come. However, those who build on solid rock can withstand anything that comes their way. Let us all make God, the Solid Rock, our foundation.

Prayer: *Father God, help us to build our foundation on your word and to trust that with you we can withstand all circumstances. Amen*

Thought for the day: Today I will build a strong foundation through prayer and worship.

Robert Cornell (Indiana, US)

Calling out

Read Psalm 130:1–6

Seek the Lord while he may be found, call upon him while he is near.
Isaiah 55:6 (NRSV)

It can be hard to ask for help, but sometimes we have no choice. Once my dad decided to repair a bedroom radiator valve by himself. Mum was out shopping, but on her return she heard Dad calling out from the bedroom, 'Help! Help!' Dad was kneeling beside the radiator with his thumb pushed hard over the valve to stop the water from spurting out and soaking the bedroom carpet. Dad needed someone to help him and to call a plumber. He couldn't do it alone; he needed to cry out for help.

God encourages us to call out for help – to cry, shout or moan. I know that I can be reluctant to ask for the help I need, and my resistance is often self-defeating. But Isaiah 55:6 reminds us to call upon God. God has no conditions or limitations – we can call anytime, anywhere. What is stopping us? God is near, extending an open invitation to us all.

Prayer: *Heavenly Father, help us to draw near to you and to trust that you will answer when we call out for help, as we pray, 'Our Father in heaven, hallowed be your name, your kingdom come, your will be done, on earth as it is in heaven. Give us today our daily bread. And forgive us our debts, as we also have forgiven our debtors. And lead us not into temptation, but deliver us from the evil one.'* Amen*

Thought for the day: God hears when I call.

Hilary Allen (Somerset, United Kingdom)

Don't give up

Read Romans 5:1–5

We do not lose heart. Though outwardly we are wasting away, yet inwardly we are being renewed day by day.

2 Corinthians 4:16 (NIV)

According to my high school sports teacher, the worst thing you could do as a runner was to drop out of a race or be disqualified. One year I was at the regional athletics meeting where I had a chance to qualify for the national championships. I was really feeling the pressure – my legs were shaking on the starting line. I ran well for the first two laps of the race, and I knew I could pass the runner in front of me. But when it was time to move ahead, I felt even more pressure. Instead of passing my competitor, I fell off the side of the track. I was disqualified. I usually tell people that I think I fainted, but in reality I simply panicked and quit.

Paul knew that running the race of faith isn't always easy. There are challenges in following Jesus and even in just being human. But in today's quoted verse, Paul tells us not to give up.

After the race, my sports teacher was disappointed. But then he said, 'Let's focus on the next race.' That made me want to try again, and I never gave up on another race. My teacher's words remind me of the way God never loses faith in us. No matter what storms we're going through or what past experiences haunt us, God is drawing closer and will never leave. He never gives up on us.

Prayer: *Dear God, thank you for never giving up on us. Give us the strength to continue running the race, even when we are tired or afraid. Amen*

Thought for the day: God never gives up on me.

Adam Benson (North Carolina, US)

God still amazes

Read Luke 2:8–14

In that region there were shepherds living in the fields, keeping watch over their flock by night. Then an angel of the Lord stood before them, and the glory of the Lord shone around them, and they were terrified.
Luke 2:8–9 (NRSV)

Not long ago I was so amazed by a sunrise that I rushed out of the back door in my pyjamas with camera in hand. I wanted to capture a photograph before the colours faded. I was so captivated by the beauty that I didn't stop to think about what I looked like.

If I was so amazed by a sunrise, I try to imagine the amazement of the shepherds in today's reading. That night outside Bethlehem, as the shepherds were ready to drift off to sleep, suddenly an angel of the Lord appeared. They were more than amazed – they were terrified! But I think their most amazing encounter that night was not with the angel but with the baby to whom they were sent. After they had found Jesus lying in a manger, just as the angel had told them, they went out praising and glorifying God.

That night long ago was not just about angels, shepherds and innkeepers. That night was about a message from God that was wrapped in swaddling cloths. The message was and is Jesus Christ, who has come to show us the very picture of God!

Prayer: *O God, make us ready to share the good news of great joy with the people around us today. We pray in Jesus' name. Amen*

Thought for the day: There's great joy in watching for God's surprises!

Peter Caligiuri (Florida, US)

Words of encouragement

Read Joshua 1:1–11

'Be strong and courageous. Do not be afraid; do not be discouraged, for the Lord your God will be with you wherever you go.'
Joshua 1:9 (NIV)

When my friend was asked to become a song leader in our Christian fellowship, she asked me, 'Can I do this?' To encourage her, I said, 'Yes, you can!' Despite her hesitations, she can now lead us well.

In today's Bible reading, God encouraged Joshua. Several times God said to him, 'Be strong and courageous!' Leading the Israelites in Moses' place was not an easy task. As Joshua carried out his new duty to lead the people into the land of Canaan, he was probably afraid. But when he heard God's words of encouragement, his spirit awoke and his strength rose. Joshua then ordered the officers of the people to prepare to take possession of the land God had promised to them.

Like he did for Joshua, God gives us words of encouragement. Whenever we feel our duties or responsibilities are heavy beyond our strength, he whispers to us, 'Be strong and courageous!' Because he knows each of us, we can trust that if God says we are capable of something, then we are!

Prayer: *God Almighty, thank you for encouraging us when we feel afraid and inadequate. Help us always to listen to you and to trust your guidance for our lives. Amen*

Thought for the day: Just as God encourages me, I can encourage others.

Linawati Santoso (East Java, Indonesia)

PRAYER FOCUS: SOMEONE WHO FEELS DISCOURAGED

Undeserving

Read Luke 6:27–36

Do not repay evil with evil or insult with insult. On the contrary, repay evil with blessing, because to this you were called so that you may inherit a blessing.
1 Peter 3:9 (NIV)

The lab director was often difficult to get on with. She seemed bent on getting me fired, and with each new disagreement our conflict intensified. She and my other colleagues also butted heads often. Finally, after years of friction in our workplace, she resigned from her job.

As she struggled to pack all her belongings, I watched in amazement as a Christian colleague – who had also had a difficult relationship with the director – began to help her pack.

Initially I thought, 'What has she done to deserve any kindness?' But that led me to consider, 'What have I done to deserve the grace shown to me by the Lord?' I remembered Abigail and her grace that softened David's heart (see 1 Samuel 25:2-42). I also remembered Peter, who denied knowing Jesus after his arrest. Yet Jesus forgave him (see Luke 22:54–62; John 21:15–19). And today's quoted scripture verse reminds us that we are all called to bless those who do evil to us.

Thinking on these things, I returned to my question: 'What have I done to merit God's forgiveness?' Nothing. So how could I question the lab director's merit in receiving even this smallest gesture of grace? I rose from my desk and helped her pack.

Prayer: *Dear Lord Jesus, thank you for forgiving us. Give us strength to follow your example of showing mercy. Amen*

Thought for the day: What would it look like to bless those who curse me?

Steve Smith (Texas, US)

God's helping hands

Read Psalm 146:5–10

The Lord watches over the foreigner and sustains the fatherless and the widow.
Psalm 146:9 (NIV)

One year as the Christmas season approached, some talented seamstresses created a set of costumes for the children of our church to wear in the annual nativity play. The garments were well made and quite realistic. The nativity play was a great success, and I looked forward to using the costumes at Sunday school for years to come.

After Christmas was over, a church member volunteered to launder the outfits and bring them back to be packed away. Because of a mix-up, the costumes ended up on a rack of giveaway clothing at the food bank we hold every week for people in the community. Many of the guests were delighted with the clothing and received the items gratefully. At the end of the day, not a single garment was left.

When I first heard that our costumes were gone, I was upset about the mistake. But then I realised that God had used our church to meet a need. How humbling it is to be a part of God's work in the world!

Prayer: *Dear God, help us always to be aware of the needs of others and to do everything we can to meet those needs. Amen*

Thought for the day: Even when I am unaware, God can use me to meet the needs of others.

Betsy Mitchell (New York, US)

Imperfect but useful

Read 2 Timothy 2:20–25

Those who cleanse themselves… will be instruments for special purposes, made holy, useful to the Master and prepared to do any good work.
2 Timothy 2:21 (NIV)

Sometimes it seems unlikely that God would use me in his divine plan. How could someone as insignificant as me be of use to the creator of the universe?

Yet because of God's grace for me, I have wanted to serve him above all else. As my faith has grown, I have felt that God has a purpose for me in different situations – like being of help to someone who has no one else to turn to.

At times we may think it's unlikely that God could use us to accomplish his will. We may expect someone more kind, gentle or loving to be his instrument in the world – and in our neighbourhood. Yet God can use us, whoever and wherever we are. The apostle Paul writes that Christians are 'instruments for special purposes, made holy, useful to the Master and prepared to do any good work'.

We are imperfect, and we live in an imperfect world. But God will use us even if we feel unworthy and unlikely. Our value to his work may not be apparent to us, but it's always clear to him.

Prayer: *God of the universe, thank you for using us for your kingdom's work. Encourage us by the power of your Holy Spirit. Amen*

Thought for the day: My efforts are always valuable to God.

Peter Veugelaers (Wellington, New Zealand)

Listening to God

Read Revelation 3:18–24

'Whoever has ears to listen should pay attention!… Listen carefully! God will evaluate you with the same standard you use to evaluate others. Indeed, you will receive even more.'
Mark 4:23–24 (CEB)

These days I have plenty of time for patio-sitting at my home in Mississippi. But life wasn't always this way. When I was 35, I struggled through a divorce and became a single mum of four children. I began getting up early in the morning so that I could have time to be alone and to listen to God.

My children are now grown up, but my early-morning time is still the most important part of my day. It is my time to listen to the open, loving heart of God. As I sit quietly, a bird chirps, leaves rustle or raindrops pummel the roof. Once, as the sun rose, it cast a shadow in the shape of a cross on my cedar fence. As I see and hear God's presence in these sights and sounds, I open my heart to his love.

From my years of talking with my heavenly Father, I now listen to others differently. Behind their words, I often hear broken, sad and anxious hearts that sound a lot like mine did. I listen to their hearts because God has always heard mine.

Through pain, busyness, anxiety and hard circumstances in my life, when I listened to God's heart, I felt him listening to mine and blessings flowed.

Prayer: *Dear God, thank you for teaching us how to listen to you. Help us to hear the hearts of others and to show them your love and care. Amen*

Thought for the day: How can I listen to others the way God listens to me?

Sarah Randall (Mississippi, US)

Working with Jesus

Read 2 Corinthians 9:6–15

A generous person will be enriched, and one who gives water will get water.
Proverbs 11:25 (NRSV)

During one of my first mission trips to Mexico, we stayed in the minister's home next to the church and worked alongside the people in the community. Although the trip was nearly 30 years ago, I recall one Wednesday as if it were yesterday.

While we worked, an elderly woman came to the nearby community well. She filled two buckets with water, and then carefully placed them on a yoke across her shoulders. After just a few steps along the rocky path home, she stumbled and fell, spilling the water. A member from our team rushed down off his ladder. He helped her up, brushed dirt off her, refilled her buckets and carried them to her home.

During a church service that evening, when we were asked to share where we had seen Christ that week, one man told about painting with Jesus, another said he did carpentry with Jesus and then the elderly woman recounted how Jesus helped with her water. That experience continues to live with me as I ask daily, 'How am I being Jesus for others?'

Prayer: *Dear God, thank you that even simple acts can be performed in Jesus' name. Help us to share your love continuously with others. Amen*

Thought for the day: Who has reflected Jesus' love to me lately?

Griffith Harlow (North Carolina, US)

Immanuel

Read Isaiah 7:10–14

'The virgin will conceive and give birth to a son, and will call him Immanuel.'
Isaiah 7:14 (NIV)

Each Christmas season I spend time reading and rereading the Christmas story from the Bible. This year the story provided a particularly relevant truth. A month before Christmas, several family issues surfaced, and it seemed I would be spending much of the holiday season alone. A friend and I had planned a quiet evening together a few days before Christmas, but then my friend cancelled our plans because of a death in the family.

Early on 23 December, I awoke and began asking God why I had to be alone this Christmas. I told God about how most of my family members were so busy with personal issues that I wouldn't get to see them, and that my close friend would no longer be available. During my fervent conversation with God, the word 'Immanuel' surfaced, along with its meaning, 'God with us'. Instantly I understood the deeper meaning of Christmas. We love to have friends and family around for Christmas. But the greater celebration is that God in Christ came to be with each of us so that we are never alone.

Prayer: *Lord God, when we feel lonely, remind us of your constant presence with us – not only at Christmas but at all times. Amen*

Thought for the day: Christmas is about God's gift of love in Jesus.

Steven Thompson (Iowa, US)

A transforming moment

Read 1 Corinthians 15:50–58

My dear brothers and sisters, stand firm. Let nothing move you.
Always give yourselves fully to the work of the Lord, because you know
that your labour in the Lord is not in vain.
1 Corinthians 15:58 (NIV)

My parents serve in several Christian communities, and they always take me with them to help in their ministry. Some time ago I began to feel that working in those communities was not for me. I told my parents that I was not invested in the work and did not feel the presence of God.

My father responded by telling me that the most important part of ministry is to serve God and share the good news with others. He asked that I think about this purpose and reconsider my point of view. I felt frustrated and angry. I felt that serving God was becoming a burden for me.

Two days later while I was listening to music, a Christian song started playing. I closed my eyes as I listened. In that moment I felt a strong presence and heard the words, 'Serve me with gladness.' It was a transforming moment that I cannot fully explain, but God was with me in my time of doubt. That moment filled me with joy and inspired in me a genuine desire to continue working with my parents in community outreach ministries to share the good news of Jesus Christ.

Prayer: *Spirit of the living God, thank you for standing by us in our moments of doubt. Inspire us to live as true disciples and to use our voices to share your message with others. Amen*

Thought for the day: Even in times of doubt, God stands with me.

Carolina Murgueytio (Pichincha, Ecuador)

Why worry?

Read Matthew 6:25–34

'Do not worry about your life… Can any of you by worrying add a single hour to your span of life?'
Matthew 6:25, 27 (NRSV)

I worry about almost everything. When I feel overcome by worry, I look for signs of inspiration to help me cope. I found such inspiration in a most unlikely place this morning as I went out to walk our dog. A small bird was sleeping in a corner of the porch. He was dry and safe and brought to my mind the scripture reading for today.

Jesus tells us not to worry. He tells us to look at the birds, which never sow or reap because they are taken care of by God. I hope to become more trusting and to worry less, especially about things that I cannot control. A loving, caring God looks over me and takes every step that I take. God has helped me deal with the effects of war, a devastating tornado and many other challenges.

I am now in my mid-70s, and I know that my future and all the worries that burden me are in God's hands. I am confident that he will care for me always.

I look forward each morning to seeing the little bird – a bird that Jesus says can remind me to cast my worries on God, who is the giver of peace and joy.

Prayer: *Giver of peace and joy, help us to cast our worries on you and to be faithful no matter what difficulties may come. In Jesus' name. Amen*

Thought for the day: What reminders help me to stop worrying and trust God?

Harold Lemley (Georgia, US)

A daughter's gift

Read Deuteronomy 7:7–9

The Lord your God is the only true God… who keeps the covenant and proves loyal to everyone who loves him.
Deuteronomy 7:9 (CEB)

When my daughter was young, her school held a Christmas fair. One of the highlights was a stall where the children could select their own gifts for their parents and other relatives. Though mums and dads were not allowed in the room, I remember sneaking a look to see my daughter choose her presents for her dad, her brother and me.

On Christmas morning she could hardly wait to hand me my gift. As she presented it to me, she proudly said, 'I picked this out all by myself for you, Mummy!' I opened my present and saw a little green frog sitting on a rocking chair, reading a newspaper with the headline: 'World's Greatest Grandpa'! I loved it immediately. To this day, some 25 years later, that little frog sits on a shelf in my dining room.

I think God probably feels similar delight when we offer our gifts of serving his children or spending time in prayer and worship. Our efforts may not be perfect, but when we offer them in love, God receives them joyfully. That little frog is a reminder to me of my love for my daughter and God's love for me.

Prayer: *Dear God, thank you for the love that you so freely give to us, your children. May we always stay faithful to you in everything that we say and do. Amen*

Thought for the day: God delights in my imperfect gifts.

Andrea Woronick (Connecticut, US)

Working together

Read Romans 12:1–8

By the grace given to me I say to everyone among you not to think of yourself more highly than you ought to think, but to think with sober judgement, each according to the measure of faith that God has assigned.
Romans 12:3 (NRSV)

I once read that the most successful leaders are those who realise their gifts and their limitations. Paul warns us not to think too highly of ourselves by assuming we can do everything on our own, and he uses himself as an example.

If anyone could have thought highly of himself, it was Paul. Paul was an educated man; he had been a lawyer, politician and Pharisee. Yet, in spite of all his abilities and accomplishments, he admitted he needed the support of others to accomplish his work for Christ. Paul knew his strengths and appreciated that others could build on what he had begun.

Paul writes that we must use sound judgement in our opinion of ourselves. We must think clearly about our limitations and believe that the Lord will bring us together with people who possess different strengths to help accomplish the work God has given us. When we understand that our combined faith and qualities can work together, we each will fulfil our purpose in serving the Lord.

Prayer: *Dear Lord, help us to acknowledge both our strengths and our weaknesses and to value the gifts others bring as we do your work together. Amen*

Thought for the day: My strengths and weaknesses are part of the body of Christ.

Nelson Nwosu (Anambra, Nigeria)

A much-needed gift

Read Psalm 62:1–12

'Be still, and know that I am God.'
Psalm 46:10 (NIV)

After a long day at work, I accidentally locked my keys and my phone in my car when I stopped to get petrol.

After going into the petrol station to call my husband, I went back outside to wait. It was going to be at least 40 minutes until he could bring the spare key. At first, I was frustrated. I had 40 minutes to just sit and wait without my phone to write emails or entertain myself. Then I realised that this quiet, uninterrupted downtime was an unexpected but much-needed gift from God.

As I sat there with nothing to do, I realised how often I have unplanned quiet moments. When there is a power cut, my phone dies and I don't have a charger, my son's bus is running late or I am waiting to see the doctor, the unproductive time can seem like an inconvenience. But each quiet moment gives me the opportunity to take a deep breath, refocus my thoughts and just be with God.

Prayer: *Dear God, thank you for being with us throughout our day. Help us to recognise and appreciate moments to be still in your presence. We pray as Jesus taught us, saying, 'Our Father which art in heaven, Hallowed be thy name. Thy kingdom come. Thy will be done, as in heaven, so in earth. Give us day by day our daily bread. And forgive us our sins; for we also forgive every one that is indebted to us. And lead us not into temptation; but deliver us from evil.'* Amen

Thought for the day: When can I stop today and spend a few minutes in God's presence?

Julie Sipe (Pennsylvania, US)

Christmas blessings

Read Isaiah 43:14–21

'Do not dwell on the past. See, I am doing a new thing! Now it springs up; do you not perceive it? I am making a way in the wilderness and streams in the wasteland.'
Isaiah 43:18–19 (NIV)

Around Christmas we are encouraged to make time in our busy schedules to talk to God, spend time in meditation and read the Bible.

These are great suggestions, but my problem is that I am not busy. I am 86 years old, am estranged from my family, have macular degeneration and live alone. My Christmases are devoid of joyful activity. I used to spend the Christmas season remembering the good times spent with my family in previous years. But when I dwelled on the past, I ended up overwhelmed by tears and sadness.

Recently I have learned to turn my thoughts to the present and focus on how much God is blessing me. I live in a nice place, a grocery delivery service has started in my area, I go to a day centre for lunch a few days a week and I have time to be with God and time to write.

So instead of pining for the past, I focus on the present and anticipate the future, knowing that the Christ of Bethlehem is with me and brings blessings day by day. I still miss my family and sometimes weep over them, but I have learned that we can enjoy the present when we begin to name the blessings God has given us today. It is a never-ending list that can bring us the joy of the Christmas season.

Prayer: *Dear God, bring the fullness of your Son's birth to those who are alone. Amen*

Thought for the day: Even if I cannot recover the joys of the past, God is in the present.

Kenneth Claar (Idaho, US)

The miracle of Christmas

Read John 1:15–18

'Look, the virgin shall conceive and bear a son, and they shall name him Emmanuel,' which means, 'God is with us.'
Matthew 1:23 (NRSV)

As a minister's wife, I have helped with many Christmas nativity plays over the years. Memories abound of wise men with cardboard crowns, shepherds in striped robes, and angels with paper wings and tinsel halos. But the play that touched my heart most was the time we had a real baby play the part of Jesus. The infant must have been no more than a few months old. The young girl who played Mary held the baby gingerly on her lap, willing the child not to cry or wiggle out of her grasp.

As I stood behind the scene looking at that infant, the power and mystery of what God accomplished so long ago touched me in a whole new way. God, the creator of the universe, chose to become part of our human family as a helpless infant needing to be cared for and loved. Just as a baby brings joy and hope to new parents, Jesus brought hope to all humanity by revealing the depth of God's love for us. As John 1:18 proclaims, 'No one has ever seen God. It is God the only Son, who is close to the Father's heart, who has made him known.' That is the miracle of Christmas: Jesus has come to show us the perfect image of God!

Prayer: *Fill our hearts, O God, with thanksgiving and praise for the gift of your Son, Jesus. Amen*

Thought for the day: Because of Jesus, we know how much God loves us.

Nancy J. Clark (Michigan, US)

A new perspective

Read Luke 2:1–7

The angel said to [the shepherds], 'Do not be afraid; for see – I am bringing you good news of great joy for all the people.'
Luke 2:10 (NRSV)

Christmas this year was different from previous seasons. I wasn't singing with a choir, so I wasn't busy with rehearsals. Most of my family members and relatives couldn't come for Christmas, so I didn't prepare a big meal but went out for dinner instead. I did a little shopping, but it was not as hectic as other years.

The most significant difference was that when I went to a Christmas service at church, I sat with other worshippers rather than with the choir. I followed along with the service in serenity and solemnly listened to the sermon. Tears fell from my eyes when we sang 'O Holy Night' and lit candles. I felt peaceful and grateful.

For a long time, Christmas was just an annual tradition with to-do lists and performances. This year, I experienced Christmas from another perspective as I let myself come as a person longing to see the Saviour.

Prayer: *Dear God, thank you for giving us Jesus, your Son. Amen*

Thought for the day: How am I seeking the Saviour this Christmas?

Juita Kartini (Jakarta, Indonesia)

Refuge in the storm

Read Matthew 14:28–33

Let all who take refuge in you rejoice; let them ever sing for joy. Spread your protection over them, so that those who love your name may exult in you.
Psalm 5:11 (NRSV)

A once-in-a-lifetime storm settled over a small part of the county I live in and dumped an unbelievable amount of water in a very short time. I watched as roads were closed and dramatic rescues took place. The road in front of the restaurant where my wife and I had eaten earlier that day was now a raging river. The restaurant itself was now a refuge for people pulled from the flood.

The flooding reminded me of how unpredictable and tenuous life can be. We expect things to go smoothly. We want to believe that we can handle the situations we encounter. But deep down, we know that something may come along to overwhelm us. Our storms may appear in a hospital ward or around a kitchen table looking at a pile of bills or as we are talking with a child who has been bullied at school. Where do we go to find our refuge?

I will admit there are times I have tried to face my storms with my own strength and willpower – we all do. It is in these moments that we need to reach for God, the refuge the psalmist speaks of. And when we reach for him, we discover that our loving God is already reaching for us.

Prayer: *O God, the depth of your love is beyond our imagination. Help us to remember that we are never alone. Amen*

Thought for the day: I will let my challenges remind me to take refuge in God's love.

Robert Sorozan (Pennsylvania, US)

Opportunities everywhere

Read Colossians 4:2–6

Be wise in the way you act towards outsiders; make the most of every opportunity.
Colossians 4:5 (NIV)

After the church service one Sunday, a young woman behind me tapped my shoulder. She told me she was visiting our church and that throughout the service, she had sensed God telling her that the woman in front of her would pray with her. I was not going to let this opportunity pass me by. She told me of her need, and we held hands and prayed.

Praying with and for people is one way to reach others for Christ, but it's not the only way. Maybe a local food bank is in need of donations. Perhaps someone you know just returned home from the hospital and could use a meal or two. A new family may have moved in next door, and a warm welcome could help them feel at home. Opportunities to show God's love are all around us – we just need to be attuned to them.

I still periodically pray for the woman from church and her request. It would be nice to know how that prayer may be answered, but I don't need to know. I do know that when we reach out to others with God's love, he will handle the rest. In the meantime, we can be alert and 'make the most of every opportunity' that God places in our path.

Prayer: *Dear Lord, help us to be aware of the opportunities you place before us. Please give us the courage to respond and share your love. Amen*

Thought for the day: Prayer is a way I can show God's love to those around me.

Lorraine Baldus (Michigan, US)

Character first

Read 1 Samuel 16:1–13

'The Lord does not look at the things people look at. People look at the outward appearance, but the Lord looks at the heart.'
1 Samuel 16:7 (NIV)

Almost 900 miles from home on a motorcycle trip, we rolled into a small town in Wyoming and found a nice motel. It was a cool day, so we were wearing our leather gear, including chaps and bandanas. Some of us were unshaven, and I'm sure those in the motel heard our motorcycles coming. We looked like rough bikers, but we didn't think anything of it.

When a few of us went into the lobby, the manager quoted what seemed like an extremely high price for the rooms and said it was not negotiable. We stepped away from the counter to talk it over, but not before he had glimpsed the shocked looks on our faces. 'Come back over here,' the manager said. 'I tell you what. I'll give you a discount on one condition: you promise not to trash the place.' We agreed, and later we all had a good laugh.

Our biker appearance sometimes seems to instil fear in people. But when we look only at outward appearances, we can be fooled. To people, David didn't look like a king. He didn't look like a warrior when he faced Goliath either, but God saw his potential. People look at the outward appearance, but God looks at the heart. Wouldn't it be great if we could see people through God's eyes?

Prayer: *Dear God, thank you for seeing our hearts. Help us to avoid judging others by their outward appearances. Amen*

Thought for the day: Today I will try to see others as God sees them.

Bill McConnell (Kansas, US)

Mercy pick

Read Ephesians 2:1–10

Brothers and sisters, you are loved by God, and we know that he has chosen you.
1 Thessalonians 1:4 (CEB)

I still remember to this day the feeling of standing in the gym at school, waiting to be chosen by one of the two team captains. Straightaway, others more athletically gifted were picked. I watched with a sense of dread as the numbers dwindled and I remained, unchosen and unwanted. At last my name was called, only because the team captains had no other choice.

On a few rare occasions, though, I was not one of the last ones picked. If one of my friends was selected to be a team captain, she would always choose me sooner than my skills warranted. Her love for me led her to choose me so I wouldn't be one of the last chosen. I was a 'mercy pick', spared from the humiliation of feeling unwanted.

This is how God chooses me. God's choosing isn't based on my skills, abilities or behaviour, but on his mercy – out of love for me in spite of my weaknesses. My goodness is not my own but God's. I need to remain mindful of this truth as I look at others, because in God's eyes we are all mercy picks. We are all chosen because of how loving God is and not because of how good we are.

Prayer: *Loving Father, thank you for showing us mercy beyond measure. Help us to extend to others the mercy we have received. Amen*

Thought for the day: How can I show mercy to others as God has shown mercy to me?

Shirla Andes (Indiana, US)

God's beautiful creation

Read Psalm 134:1–3

May the Lord bless you from Zion, he who is the Maker of heaven and earth.

Psalm 134:3 (NIV)

A recent retreat I attended included a Sunday worship service that took place shortly after sunrise. I am not accustomed to rising so early on Sundays, so I was not looking forward to it. However, as I walked up the hill and saw the sun rising above a mountain ridge, I was stunned by the beauty of the view. The reflection of the sun's brilliant rays made the surface of the sea look like a golden mirror, with birds gliding effortlessly over the surface. The cool breeze of the morning air refreshed me even more than coffee. My annoyance at getting up early was replaced by an incredible sense of peace.

Meditating and praying in church is one of the ways that I find peace and rest in my everyday life. But the beauty and wonder of God's creation remind me that we can find sanctuary in every corner of the earth. The Lord of all creation hears our prayers and has blessed us with the abundant beauty and resources of the earth, but we often fail to appreciate them. God's blessings are everywhere, and he is with us in every moment.

Prayer: *Dear Lord, thank you for the blessing of this beautiful earth. Prompt us to be still in the busyness of our lives and to appreciate your blessings. Amen*

Thought for the day: I can enjoy God's creation any time.

John Jen-Chiang (Hong Kong, China)

Always

Read Joshua 4:1–7

'Remember, I am with you always, to the end of the age.'
Matthew 28:20 (NRSV)

I was driving our church bus, taking some of our older members on a day trip. When we travel, we have a backup SUV following us in case of a bus problem or a passenger emergency. As usual we made a stop at a restaurant along the way.

As we were leaving, I wanted to be sure the SUV was behind us. However, I couldn't see it in my side-view mirrors, and the bus had no rear-view mirror. I thought maybe the driver had not started yet or had gone on ahead of me. I circled around the restaurant twice looking for the SUV, but it was nowhere to be seen. Finally, I called the driver and asked, 'Where are you?' He answered, 'I'm right behind you, and I'm wondering why we keep circling the restaurant!' He was there with me all the time!

Even though I cannot see God, I trust his promises. My trust is strengthened by remembering the many times I've seen God's grace at work in my life. Sometimes his presence is apparent only in looking back on my life, so I find it helpful to remember the ways he has helped me in the past. Even when it is difficult to feel God's presence, he promises to be with us always.

Prayer: *Ever-present God, thank you for your promise always to be with us. During hard times, help us to remember your faithfulness to us. Amen*

Thought for the day: When have I most recently sensed God's presence?

Bob Peterson (Texas, US)

Small group questions

Wednesday 2 September

1 Is there anyone in your life whom you have been avoiding? How might you get in contact with them in the coming week?

2 When have you felt God encouraging you to do something you didn't really want to do? How did you respond? What did you learn from the experience?

3 Which scripture passages remind you of the importance of remaining open to new people and showing God's love to others? How do you apply what you read in those passages to your life?

4 When have you missed an opportunity to love others? What are some practical steps you can take to become more aware of every opportunity?

5 How do you think your church might be transformed if every member sought to show God's love to those who are drastically different from them?

Wednesday 9 September

1 How does spending time reading scripture strengthen your relationship with God? In what ways does it make you feel more equipped to serve God?

2 Have there been times in your life when you struggled to discern your calling from God? Which scripture passages encouraged you or brought you clarity during those times?

3 Do you find it easier to hear what God is trying to tell you when you purposefully spend time with him? Why or why not?

4 Name some specific ways you could draw closer to God. In what ways could these new practices transform your faith and your life?

5 Who or what helps you remain consistent in your current spiritual practices? What role does your church play in your spiritual life?

Wednesday 16 September

1 Today's writer found that her appreciation for beauty has changed over the years. Where have you noticed a similar change in your own mind? What can you learn from that shift?

2 What does it mean to you that we are ever-evolving creations? What does that teach you about the God who created us?

3 Do you find yourself worried about the future or the changes you may undergo as you age? Which prayers, Bible verses or people help you to release those worries?

4 Which biblical characters demonstrate how a person can reflect God regardless of age, abilities or past actions? How do their examples encourage you?

5 What can you do to ensure that your actions reflect God's power and presence in your life? What is the importance of reflecting God to others?

Wednesday 23 September

1 Do you have a prayer partner? If so, in what ways does this person encourage your spiritual life? If you do not, where do you find encouragement in your faith?

2 Do you prefer prayers that follow a certain ritual, or do you enjoy praying conversationally? In what ways are those prayer experiences different? What new prayer practice would you like to try?

3 How does prayer strengthen your connection to God? When do you feel the most connected to others through prayer?

4 What role do your friends play in your spiritual life? In what ways can you encourage someone else's faith today?

5 How does your church intentionally try to 'quench the thirst' of those in your community? How do you participate in those efforts? In what ways can you encourage others to participate?

Wednesday 30 September

1 When have you let negative thoughts or expectations prevent you from enjoying an experience? Which scripture passages encourage you in such times?

2 What 'signs' have you put up that invite fear into your life? Does Jesus' call to the disciples make you want to drop your 'signs'? Why or why not?

3 Do you find it easy to rejoice in the journey of your life? If so, why? If not, what spiritual practices might help you to embrace your journey more joyfully?

4 What prayer practices bring you comfort when you find your mind overcome with negative or fearful thoughts?

5 Who or what helps you drop your 'signs'? How would you encourage someone who is struggling to drop their 'signs'?

Wednesday 7 October

1 Describe a time in your faith journey when you 'cast your line into the shadows'. What was your experience of trusting God to provide as you took a leap of faith?

2 Do you ever feel like it would be easier to stick to your routine than to speak about and act on your faith? What biblical or historical figures serve as examples to you of boldly living out their faith? How can you strive to be more like them?

3 What risks have you taken for your faith? Where in your life do you see the fruits of following Christ? What makes you willing to take risks for what you believe?

4 In what ways are you encouraged to know that the Lord promises us the crown of life if we persevere in our faith? Which scripture passages help you persevere during difficult times?

5 Who in your faith community encourages you to live your faith boldly? What can you do to encourage others in your faith community to be bold as well?

Wednesday 14 October

1 When have you been so preoccupied that you struggled to understand someone? What can you do to refocus your attention when you realise that you are not truly hearing others?

2 Do you ever find it difficult to hear God's message when you read scripture? What helps you be attentive to God's word and message as you read?

3 Describe a time when you did not feel that others heard or understood you. How did you respond? What did that experience teach you about how you want to treat others?

4 What does it mean to you to have a receptive heart that listens to the needs of others? Why do you think it is important that Christians pay attention to others? In what ways could you grow in this area?

5 How does your church listen to the needs of others? How could your church better focus on others? In what ways do you think your church is reflecting God's love and bearing fruit?

Wednesday 21 October

1 Do you worry a lot? Which scripture passages, spiritual practices, people, exercises or activities help you to find peace when you are full of worry or sadness?

2 Have you ever prayed scripture? If so, which scripture passages appear in your prayers most frequently? If not, in what ways would you like to incorporate scripture into your prayer life?

3 When is prayer most comforting for you? Does prayer ever feel unhelpful? What other practices help you during difficult times?

4 Do you have a fear or worry that has stopped resurfacing thanks to your faith? If so, why do you think that happened? If not, in what ways do you think creating a new faith habit might help?

5 When and where do you most clearly notice God's peace? What does God's peace feel like for you? How can you share God's peace with those around you?

Wednesday 28 October

1 Describe a time when you have been disappointed or angry because a dream did not come to fruition. Did you ever doubt God's plans for you? What helped you find direction?

2 Does it encourage you to know that God's plans for you may be bigger than your plans for yourself, or do you find that difficult to accept at times? What brings you comfort about your future?

3 How do you serve God? Does your service look different from what you imagined? Which scripture passages remind you of the value of your service?

4 Is it sometimes hard to trust that God knows what is best for your life? When is it easy to trust, and when is it difficult? What helps you when you are struggling to trust God's plans?

5 Today's writer says, 'Here I am, God. Use me.' What would it look like for you to live out that statement? How could your church change if all its members lived in that way? What can you do to embrace this attitude and encourage your faith community to do the same?

Wednesday 4 November

1 Describe a time when your relationship with God was deepened because you cared for others. How does that experience motivate you to continue caring for others?

2 How do you make sure that your spirit is in alignment with God and that you are in good relationship with others? How do those alignments help you stand firm in your faith?

3 What people or practices act as your spiritual plumb and level? What habits do you have that threaten to throw you out of alignment with God or with others? How do your plumb and level help you overcome those things?

4 What does it mean to you to live in the Spirit? How have you been blessed by the guiding of the Spirit?

5 Whom can you strengthen your relationship with today? How can you show God's love to that person?

Wednesday 11 November

1 Do you participate in an online prayer community? How does praying with that community differ from praying with others face to face?

2 When have you experienced the faithfulness of a true friend? How do you remain present in the lives of your friends and loved ones even if you can't be with them in person?

3 Today's writer prayed for her friend to be blessed with Christ's spirit of eternal life. Have you ever prayed a similar prayer? How do you remain faithful in the face of sadness like this?

4 When have you seen prayer extend beyond all boundaries? How are you encouraged by that experience?

5 Which scripture passages remind you of the importance of staying faithful to those you love? What passages encourage you to continue to pray in difficult times?

Wednesday 18 November

1 When have you felt underappreciated and unsupported? How did you react in that situation? Who or what helped you through that time?

2 A thank-you card changed the writer's attitude. When has a kind gesture changed your attitude? How has that experience changed the way you show kindness to others?

3 Who in scripture serves as an example for you of spurring others towards love and good deeds? In what ways do you try to follow their example?

4 Today's writer lists several ways you can spur someone on. List some other ways you have effectively encouraged others. How does your church show appreciation to volunteers and leaders?

5 Who needs encouragement and appreciation from you today? What kind word or gesture can you offer them? How can you make a habit of encouraging others daily?

Wednesday 25 November

1 What spiritual and physical goals do you try to achieve daily? How do you feel when you fall short of your goals? How do you feel when you achieve your goals?

2 How do you know when you are walking closely with God and when you are following your own agenda? Who or what brings you back to walking with God when you have strayed?

3 Are you encouraged to know that every day is a clean slate in your service with God, or do you find that disheartening? Why?

4 Which prayers, spiritual practices, scripture passages and people help you to align your steps with God's? What blessings do you gain when you follow God's guidance?

5 How does your faith community encourage you to accomplish your goals and to walk closely with God? How do you encourage others in your community to do the same?

Wednesday 2 December

1 Have you ever let something fall into disrepair? Were you able to refurbish it? What can this teach you about your faith?

2 Describe an object you feel best symbolises your journey of faith. Why did you choose this object?

3 Today's writer describes how having a wrought-iron frame of growing up in a faithful home helped him return to his faith. What makes up the framework of your faith? How has that framework helped you in your life?

4 How does your Christian community shape your life? What other influences shape your life?

5   In what ways can you reach out and help someone who is working to rebuild their faith? What encouragement would you give to someone who is rebuilding their faith?

Wednesday 9 December

1   How do you respond when you are under a lot of pressure? Do you ever want to give up? What helps you to persevere and stay calm?

2   What challenges have you experienced in following Jesus? What spiritual practices help you to feel renewed each day?

3   How do you feel, knowing that God never gives up on us? Which scripture passages help you remember this? When you feel abandoned, what helps remind you that God is with you?

4   What biblical characters continued running the race despite being tired or afraid? Where did they find their strength? What can you learn from them?

5   Today's writer was encouraged by his sports teacher to focus on the next race. Who in your life helps you look past your mistakes and move forward in confidence? How can you help others to do the same?

Wednesday 16 December

1   When have you had the opportunity to serve alongside the people of a community? What did you learn from that experience and from the people there?

2   Where have you seen Christ this week? How have you been blessed by that example?

3   What simple acts have you performed in the name of Jesus recently? How do those small acts reflect the love of God?

4   In what ways do you reflect Christ's love to others? How do you use the opportunities God places before you to be Jesus to someone?

5   In what ways does your church reflect Jesus' love to those outside your congregation? In what ways do people in your broader community reflect Jesus' love to you and your congregation?

Wednesday 23 December

1 Are you busy during this Christmas season, or do you have extra time on your hands? If you are busy, how do you make time to rest and be with God? If you are not busy at the moment, how can you use your spare time to grow closer to God?

2 Do you find it difficult to avoid dwelling on the past? What helps you to focus on the present and the future? How does your faith help you move on from the past?

3 How is God blessing you today? For which of these blessings are you most grateful? Why?

4 What scripture passages help you to embrace the present and give you hope for the future? Why do those passages encourage you?

5 What does it mean to you to experience the fullness of Jesus' birth? How can you share the hope and joy of Christmas with those who are alone this year?

Wednesday 30 December

1 Describe a time when you did something you were not accustomed to or did not want to do, but in which you ended up finding great joy. What did you learn from that experience?

2 What activities help you to enjoy and appreciate the beauty of God's creation? How can you find new ways to enjoy the beauty around you today?

3 Today's writer often finds peace and rest while meditating and praying in church. When and where do you most often find peace and rest?

4 What prayers and spiritual practices prompt you to be still? How do you take time to notice God's blessings around you?

5 How do you incorporate nature into your faith? What does the beauty and wonder of God's creation teach you about God, yourself and the world?

Journal page

Journal page

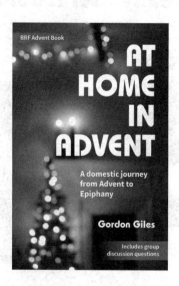

Following on from the success of *At Home in Lent*, Gordon Giles takes
a journey through Advent to Christmas and beyond in the company
of familiar seasonal and domestic objects and experiences. Focusing
on the everyday stuff we typically associate with this time of year,
including some things not so festive, he reflects on their spiritual
significance, meaning and message in today's world. Beginning with
chapters on journeying and travel, the book moves though major
Advent themes of expectation, waiting, mortality and hope to the joy
of incarnation and salvation.

At Home in Advent
A domestic journey from Advent to Epiphany
Gordon Giles
978 0 85746 980 9 £8.99
brfonline.org.uk

Really Useful Guides

Each **Really Useful Guide** focuses on a specific biblical book, making it come to life for the reader, enabling them to understand the message and to apply its truth to today's circumstances. Though not a commentary, it gives valuable insight into the book's message. Though not an introduction, it summarises the important aspects of the book to aid reading and application.

Genesis 1—11
Rebecca S. Watson
978 0 85746 791 1 £5.99

Genesis 12—50
Richard S. Briggs
978 0 85746 819 2 £5.99

Psalms
Simon P. Stocks
978 0 85746 731 7 £6.99

Really Useful Guides

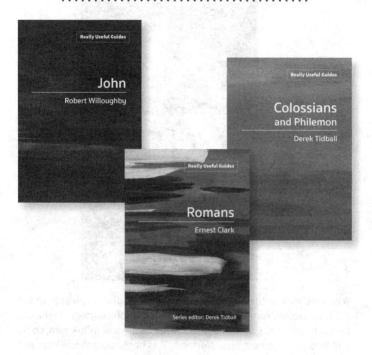

John
Robert Willoughby
978 0 85746 751 5 £5.99

Romans
Ernest Clark
978 0 85746 821 5 £5.99

**Colossians
and Philemon**
Derek Tidball
978 0 85746 730 0 £5.99

brfonline.org.uk

Develop a pattern of Bible reading, reflection & prayer

Come & See

Learning from the life of Peter

Stephen Cottrell

When we look at the life of Peter – fisherman, disciple, leader of the church – we find somebody who responded wholeheartedly to the call to 'come and see'. Come and meet Jesus, come and follow him, come and find your life being transformed. This book focuses on Peter, not because he is the best-known of Jesus' friends, nor the most loyal, but because he shows us what being a disciple of Jesus is actually like. *Come and See* provides 28 readings, plus comment and questions for personal response or group discussion.

Come and See – new edition
Learning from the life of Peter
Stephen Cottrell
978 1 80039 019 5 £8.99
brfonline.org.uk

![BRF] Enabling all ages to grow in faith

At BRF, we long for people of all ages to grow in faith and understanding of the Bible. That's what all our work as a charity is about.

- Our **Living Faith** range of resources helps Christians go deeper in their understanding of scripture, in prayer and in their walk with God. Our conferences and events bring people together to share this journey.

- We also want to make it easier for local churches to engage effectively in ministry and mission – by helping them bring new families into a growing relationship with God through **Messy Church** or by supporting churches as they nurture the spiritual life of older people through **Anna Chaplaincy**.

- Our **Holy Habits** resources help whole congregations grow together as disciples of Jesus, living out and sharing their faith.

- Our **Parenting for Faith** team coaches parents and others to raise God-connected children and teens, and enables churches to fully support them.

- We also offer a professional education service, **Barnabas in Schools**, giving primary schools confidence, expertise and opportunities for exploring Christianity in creative ways that engage all pupils.

Do you share our vision?

Though a significant proportion of BRF's funding is generated through our charitable activities, we are dependent on the generous support of individuals, churches and charitable trusts.

If you share our vision, would you help us to enable even more people of all ages to grow in faith? Your prayers and financial support are vital for the work that we do. You could:

- Support BRF's ministry with a regular donation;
- Support us with a one-off gift;
- Consider leaving a gift to BRF in your will (see page 152);
- Encourage your church to support BRF as part of your church's giving to home mission – perhaps focusing on a specific ministry or programme;
- Most important of all, support BRF with your prayers.

Donate at **brf.org.uk/donate** or use the form on pages 153–54.

Building a legacy: each person plays their part

Eliashib the high priest and his fellow priests went to work and rebuilt the Sheep Gate. They dedicated it and set its doors in place, building as far as the Tower of the Hundred, which they dedicated, and as far as the Tower of Hananel. The men of Jericho built the adjoining section, and Zakkur son of Imri built next to them.

NEHEMIAH 3:1–2 (NIV)

Nehemiah 3 recounts the story of the rebuilding of the walls of Jerusalem. A host of names follow in quick succession. While it's perhaps not the Bible passage I would like to be asked to read aloud at the front of church for fear of mispronunciation, this chapter is one of my firm favourites from the whole of the Bible and one that I return to frequently.

The Bible affirms that each person is important, made in the image of God, and that each person in the church has a part to play. The different parts come together to make the whole, and they cannot function without each other.

I know of many who at times have felt overstretched or underappreciated in their work and ministry, perhaps feeling that no one notices. Nehemiah 3 reminds us that every stone laid, every timber cut and every work undertaken is seen by God, and he knows his workers by name.

Throughout BRF's story, our ministry has grown beyond our expectation, thanks to those who have given generously, prayed faithfully and served tirelessly without seeking recognition.

They – and you – are known by God. Thank you. Could you help support this work?

Give – Pray – Get involved

If you would like some information about leaving a gift in your will to BRF, please get in touch with us at **+44 (0)1235 462305** or **giving@brf.org.uk**.

brf.org.uk/lastingdifference

SHARING OUR VISION – MAKING A GIFT

I would like to make a gift to support BRF. Please use my gift for:

☐ BRF charity ☐ Barnabas in Schools ☐ Parenting for Faith
☐ Messy Church ☐ Anna Chaplaincy ☐ where it is most needed

Title	First name/initials	Surname

Address

	Postcode

Email

Telephone

Signature	Date

giftaid it You can add an extra 25p to every £1 you give.

Please treat as Gift Aid donations all qualifying gifts of money made

☐ today, ☐ in the past four years, ☐ and in the future.

I am a UK taxpayer and understand that if I pay less Income Tax and/or Capital Gains Tax in the current tax year than the amount of Gift Aid claimed on all my donations, it is my responsibility to pay any difference.

☐ My donation does not qualify for Gift Aid.

Please notify BRF if you want to cancel this Gift Aid declaration, change your name or home address, or no longer pay sufficient tax on your income and/or capital gains.

Please complete other side of form ➡

Please return this form to:
BRF, 15 The Chambers, Vineyard, Abingdon OX14 3FE

The Bible Reading Fellowship is a Registered Charity (233280)

SHARING OUR VISION – MAKING A GIFT

Regular giving

By Direct Debit: You can set up a Direct Debit quickly and easily at **brf.org.uk/donate**

By Standing Order: Please contact our Fundraising Administrator +44 (0)1865 319700 | **giving@brf.org.uk**

One-off donation

Please accept my gift of:

☐ £10 ☐ £50 ☐ £100 Other £ [   ]

by (*delete as appropriate*):

☐ Cheque/Charity Voucher payable to 'BRF'

☐ MasterCard/Visa/Debit card/Charity card

Name on card

Card no. [ ][ ][ ][ ] [ ][ ][ ][ ] [ ][ ][ ][ ] [ ][ ][ ][ ]

Expires end [M][M] [Y][Y] Security code* [ ][ ][ ]

*Last 3 digits on the reverse of the card
ESSENTIAL IN ORDER TO PROCESS
YOUR PAYMENT

Signature   Date

☐ I would like to leave a gift in my will to BRF.

For more information, visit **brf.org.uk/lastingdifference**

For help or advice regarding making a gift, please contact our Fundraising Administrator +44 (0)1865 319700

(FR) Registered with
FUNDRAISING
REGULATOR

☚ Please complete other side of form

Please return this form to:
BRF, 15 The Chambers, Vineyard, Abingdon OX14 3FE

BRF

The Bible Reading Fellowship is a Registered Charity (233280)

UR0320

How to encourage Bible reading in your church

BRF has been helping individuals connect with the Bible for over 90 years. We want to support churches as they seek to encourage church members into regular Bible reading.

Order a Bible reading resources pack

This pack is designed to give your church the tools to publicise our Bible reading notes. It includes:

- Sample Bible reading notes for your congregation to try.
- Publicity resources, including a poster.
- A church magazine feature about Bible reading notes.

If you require a pack to be sent outside the UK or require a specific number of sample Bible reading notes, please contact us for postage costs. More information about what the current pack contains is available on our website.

How to order and find out more

- Visit **brfonline.org.uk/resourcespack**.
- Telephone BRF on +44 (0)1865 319700 Mon–Fri 9.15–17.30.
- Write to us at BRF, 15 The Chambers, Vineyard, Abingdon OX14 3FE.

Keep informed about our latest initiatives

We are continuing to develop resources to help churches encourage people into regular Bible reading, wherever they are on their journey. Join our email list at **brfonline.org.uk/signup** to stay informed about the latest initiatives that your church could benefit from.

Subscriptions

The Upper Room is published in January, May and September.

Individual subscriptions
The subscription rate for orders for 4 or fewer copies includes postage and packing:

The Upper Room annual individual subscription   £17.85

Group subscriptions
Orders for 5 copies or more, sent to ONE address, are post free:
The Upper Room annual group subscription   £14.10

Please do not send payment with order for a group subscription. We will send an invoice with your first order.

Please note that the annual billing period for group subscriptions runs from 1 May to 30 April.

Copies of the notes may also be obtained from Christian bookshops.

Single copies of *The Upper Room* cost £4.70.

Prices valid until 30 April 2021.

Giant print version
The Upper Room is available in giant print for the visually impaired, from:

Torch Trust for the Blind
Torch House
Torch Way
Northampton Road
Market Harborough   Tel: +44 (0)1858 438260
LE16 9HL   **torchtrust.org**

THE UPPER ROOM: INDIVIDUAL/GIFT SUBSCRIPTION FORM

> **All our Bible reading notes can be ordered online by visiting
> brfonline.org.uk/collections/subscriptions**

☐ I would like to take out a subscription myself (complete your name and address details once)

☐ I would like to give a gift subscription (please provide both names and addresses)

Title .... First name/initials .... Surname ....

Address ....

.... Postcode ....

Telephone .... Email ....

Gift subscription name ....

Gift subscription address ....

.... Postcode ....

Gift message (20 words max. or include your own gift card):

....

....

Please send *The Upper Room* beginning with the January 2021 /
May 2021 / September 2021 issue (*delete as appropriate*):

Annual individual subscription ☐ £17.85   Total enclosed £ ....

Method of payment

☐ Cheque (made payable to BRF) ☐ MasterCard / Visa

Card no. ☐☐☐☐ ☐☐☐☐ ☐☐☐☐ ☐☐☐☐

Expires end [M M] [Y Y]   Security code* [ ] [ ] [ ]   Last 3 digits on the reverse of the card

*ESSENTIAL IN ORDER TO PROCESS THE PAYMENT

All our Bible reading notes can be ordered online by visiting brfonline.org.uk/collections/subscriptions

☐ Please send me .... copies of *The Upper Room* January 2021 / May 2021 / September 2021 issue (*delete as appropriate*)

Title .... First name/initials .... Surname ....

Address ....

.... Postcode ....

Telephone .... Email ....

Please do not send payment with this order. We will send an invoice with your first order.

Christian bookshops: All good Christian bookshops stock BRF publications. For your nearest stockist, please contact BRF.

Telephone: The BRF office is open Mon–Fri 9.15–17.30. To place your order, telephone +44 (0)1865 319700.

Online: brfonline.org.uk/pages/group-subscriptions

☐ Please send me a Bible reading resources pack to encourage Bible reading in my church

Please return this form with the appropriate payment to:
BRF, 15 The Chambers, Vineyard, Abingdon OX14 3FE
To read our terms and find out about cancelling your order, please visit **brfonline.org.uk/terms**.

The Bible Reading Fellowship is a Registered Charity (233280)

UR0320

To order

Online: brfonline.org.uk
Telephone: +44 (0)1865 319700 Mon–Fri 9.15–17.30

Delivery times within the UK are normally 15 working days. Prices are correct at the time of going to press but may change without prior notice.

Title	Price	Qty	Total
At Home in Advent	£8.99		
Come and See	£8.99		
Really Useful Guides: Genesis 1–11 / Genesis 12–50 / Colossians and Philemon / John / Romans – *circle selected title(s)*	£5.99		
Really Useful Guides: Psalms	£6.99		

POSTAGE AND PACKING CHARGES			
Order value	UK	Europe	Rest of world
Under £7.00	£2.00		
£7.00–£29.99	£3.00	Available on request	Available on request
£30.00 and over	FREE		

Total value of books	
Postage and packing	
Donation	
Total for this order	

Please complete in BLOCK CAPITALS

Title .... First name/initials .... Surname...

Address...

.... Postcode ....

Acc. No. .... Telephone ....

Email ....

The Bible Reading Fellowship Gift Aid Declaration *giftaid it*

Please treat as Gift Aid donations all qualifying gifts of money made

❏ today, ❏ in the past four years, ❏ and in the future **or** ❏ My donation does not qualify for Gift Aid.

I am a UK taxpayer and understand that if I pay less Income Tax and/or Capital Gains Tax in the current tax year than the amount of Gift Aid claimed on all my donations, it is my responsibility to pay any difference.

Please notify BRF if you want to cancel this declaration, change your name or home address, or no longer pay sufficient tax on your income and/or capital gains.

Method of payment

❏ Cheque (made payable to BRF) ❏ MasterCard / Visa

Card no. ⬚⬚⬚⬚ ⬚⬚⬚⬚ ⬚⬚⬚⬚ ⬚⬚⬚⬚

Expires end ⬚⬚ M M ⬚⬚ Y Y Security code* ⬚⬚⬚ Last 3 digits on the reverse of the card

Signature* .... Date .... /............ /............

*ESSENTIAL IN ORDER TO PROCESS THE PAYMENT

Please return this form to: BRF, 15 The Chambers, Vineyard, Abingdon OX14 3FE | enquiries@brf.org.uk
To read our terms and find out about cancelling your order, please visit brfonline.org.uk/terms.

The Bible Reading Fellowship (BRF) is a Registered Charity (233280)

Enabling all ages to grow in faith

Anna Chaplaincy
Barnabas in Schools
Holy Habits
Living Faith
Messy Church
Parenting for Faith

The Bible Reading Fellowship (BRF) is a Christian charity that resources individuals and churches and provides a professional education service to primary schools.

Our vision is to enable people of all ages to grow in faith and understanding of the Bible and to see more people equipped to exercise their gifts in leadership and ministry.

To find out more about our ministries and programmes, visit

brf.org.uk